How to Stop Smoking

Matthew Aldrich

Matthew Aldrich, a former smoker and self-confessed nicotine addict, has spent half of his life helping people to get where they want to be. Over the years he has worked with hundreds of clients, using various techniques to help them move on with their lives and to be smoke-free. His background in life coaching and hypnotherapy has given him the tools to get the job done. He began writing self-help books ten years ago, and this book brings together all the solutions that he has developed with successful clients.

How to Stop Smoking: 30 Solutions to Suit You

Matthew Aldrich

Acknowledgments

Thank you to everyone at Hodder for their patience and hard work, especially Victoria. Well done to Tom Haskett for the illustrations. To my father who seems to be getting younger at heart the older he gets; and to my beautiful wife and daughter Matilda, who give me a reason to smile every day.

Contents

Introduction

Let's face it! If we found out tomorrow that smoking was good for us, we smokers would be in complete smoker heaven. Our under-appreciated friend, the cigarette, could take its loyal place by our side. We would stack multiple packs next to the vitamin cupboard. We would organize cigarettes in the fruit bowl in a perfect arrangement of colour and co-ordination, maybe even adjust our exercise programme to allow for more smoke breaks. Gone would be the feelings of guilt, disappointment, frustration, denial and that nagging sensation that 'I will stop tomorrow or when things get better'. In this scientific report would be extra reassurance that smoking improves your skin, helps to build lean muscle, makes you better in bed and (if we are going for it) adds ten years to your life with every 50,000 that you smoke. SORRY: I don't think that is going to happen! Just a quick thought, though: how many of us would never have taken up smoking if it was good for us?

But how about this? You can feel stronger, more in control, more alive, free, clean, less stressed, calmer, more satisfied, able to move forward, richer, sexier, fearless, oh and definitely better in bed. All you have to do is less than what you're doing now, and understand the relationship you have with cigarettes. What's holding you back? Why has it been so hard in the past to stop? Why does it seem so hard to give up something that we know on every level is hurting us so much? Do some of us just have addictive natures? Are we better humans being a slave to something like smoking than something worse? Are our lives so empty that if we took away smoking there would not be enough left to keep us satisfied? Perhaps we consider ourselves hardened rebels with cast-iron lungs, and believe that smoking makes us stronger and different from the rest of the herd. Maybe it's because we have to control everything else in our lives and smoking is the one time we can let go and be naughty and do the decadent act of chugging gallons of smoke into our bodies. Perhaps the fear and guilt of smoking stops us having to deal with our real fears, and it is better the devil we know than another struggle we find harder to deal with. **When do you want your life to start getting better?**

We may think that we feel more satisfied as a smoker than without cigarettes. That, as smokers, in some clever way we are experiencing a magical high that non-smokers are unaware of and too weak-lunged to do. Non-smokers probably look at us and just wish they had the balls and lungs to reach the heady heights of pleasure and satisfaction that we are prepared to endure as loyal members of the nicotine gang. For every excuse we give for smoking, for every justification, for every lie we tell ourselves just ask yourself this question: 'If I could click my fingers and you could be a happy non-smoker, would you let me click my fingers?' If you honestly said 'No' then I can save you a few good hours of your life. Put this book back on the shelf and go and enjoy that feeling of denial; it's probably working really well for you in your world.

You are reading this book because you want to improve something in your life. You want to move on to better things, to accomplish more, to feel free and in control. You're tired of those days when the first thing you think about in the morning is a smoke, and you can't make the coffee quickly enough to go with that first cigarette. You're fed up with that feeling of 'I will do it tomorrow when I feel better'. You're frustrated that even though you are capable of achieving many good things, you just can't kick a bit of weed tightly packed into a rolled piece of paper. You're sick of trying and failing, and living with that disappointment. If you're a secret smoker, you are exhausted with all the cleansing and covert rituals you have to perform to hide your shame. The breath fresheners, the chewing gum, the obsessive washing of your hands. Even running into the house making out you are bursting for a pee, and in desperation using anything from mouthwash to toilet cleaner to hide your stink. (I hope that it's not just me who did that!)

Smoking continually interrupts our lives: it saps our strength, wastes our time, makes us irritable, and for some of us it gives us an excuse to hide from our full potential and stops us from succeeding.

So why can't you just say 'No'? Nothing bad is going to happen to you if you do. In fact, quite the opposite. Everything is going to get better. Your body and your brain are going to benefit in so many ways. Your health, outlook, energy, self-confidence, self-belief and strength are all going to improve. When you fully understand the things that help you and the things that hurt you, why would you want to carry on hurting yourself? Are we just too consumed by our feelings and lost in our fatalistic attitude that it is better not to try? I don't think so. The chances are that you are a positive, thoughtful, enthusiastic person who does have something to give and you are not performing to your full potential because you are somewhat lost in a cloud of smoke.

I do a lot of work helping people to move forward with their lives, whether it be in physical or mental ways. From moving on from various addictions such as smoking to losing weight and eating disorders, from climbing some stairs to running a marathon. I am most satisfied in life when I am helping people to succeed and to have a better relationship with themselves.

I certainly don't come at this from a position of piety or abstinence. As you read on, it will become clear that I struggle more than most. Sometimes I have been so badly lost that I have not been aware that 'I am in a wood', let alone 'unable to see the wood for the trees'.

As most of us know, smoking is an addiction, and it is no different from any other addiction. The nature of addiction is to create a feeling of dependence that seems hard or impossible to give up. It takes over part, if not all, of our existence and we firmly believe we cannot survive without it. Addiction to any substance creates a sense of emptiness when we are deprived of it. Although the hole that is created can be filled for a period of time when the substance or act is engaged in, the sense of emptiness soon returns. Addiction is simply a tool that lets us carry on our denial or avoidance with some sort of relief, numbing and relieving the pain, dissatisfaction or craving we have created. Is there a high to be had? Yes. Is it worth it? Well at this stage of the book you are going to have to answer that yourself. So ask yourself the question: 'Is smoking worth it?'

Is smoking addictive? Of course it is; it even says so on the pack. Smoking and the way it delivers its drug is such a clever addiction. Even the way cigarettes and tobacco are sold to and used by you is a matter of many years of cleverly planned design. Ask yourself: 'does smoking honestly satisfy you, or is it actually stopping you from doing what you really want?'.

The physical act of smoking is very easy to stop; all you have to do is not put the next cigarette in your mouth. The fact that you are reading this book means you have already accepted that this is something that you might be willing to try. To achieve that we just need to understand and deal with the chemical craving and with the mental association your brain has with smoking. The chemical craving is easy to deal with once you understand your relationship with smoking. Thankfully, when you have all the honest answers about smoking and your own solutions, stopping will be as easy as turning down a punch in the face.

Please write down these questions and answer them.

► Are you happy to carry on with things the way they are?

► If nothing changes, what will life be like in the future?

► What makes you want to stay the same?

► Is there anything holding you back?

► What is the worst that could happen in ten years' time?

► What will having a healthier body feel like?

► What will being fitter and stronger give you?

► What will happen if you did more of the things you wanted to do?

► If you started to gain control over your body, what is the first thing you would do?

► When would you like your life and body to start feeling better?

Now it is important that you take the time to be honest with your answers, so do not feel you have to rush. If you struggle to answer any of the questions, there are other exercises further on in the book that will help.

From having had my first cigarette at the age of eight at the local recreation ground, I decided at the age of 14 that it was time to pack up smoking (it only took 17 years). It was not for health or money reasons. It was because my girlfriend at the time was a non-smoker and she said that she enjoyed kissing me but not if I tasted like an ashtray. This could have serious repercussions. What if she told all the girls that kissing me was not a very pleasant experience? I could be marked for life! So I did try; I stopped going to the park, tried sitting at the front of the bus, told my smoking friends that it was in the interests of health and it had nothing to do with my new girlfriend, but after a while I turned the argument around on her and said that she was trying to control me and went off and found another girlfriend. That was my first experience of losing someone to smoking. Who knows, she may have been the love of my life and I let her slip away.

Between the ages of 14 and 20, I probably averaged giving up smoking once every two weeks. Normally this would involve three or four hours of depriving myself of a smoke, before either rummaging around in the bin for an old butt or begging someone for a cigarette with the promise that it was the last one I would ask for. By the end of the evening I would buy myself a pack of ten and tell myself it wasn't the right time to give up. I always thought that packs of ten were for people who wanted to give up smoking, but now I realize they were for kids who did not have the money to buy a pack of 20. Even worse were the shop owners near my school, who would sell individual cigarettes for 15 pence each. One time I went in to buy an individual smoke only to find out that this service was not available because it was outside term time. It wasn't worth the shopkeeper's while!

Between the ages of 20 to 30 I was probably the world's worst giver-up of smoking. At the height of my addiction to giving up, I would sometimes give up three times in a day. This would involve waking up with a positive feeling from the night before that I had smoked my last cigarette and that this was the day when I no longer smoked. On the way to the station I would pass smokers and I could feel my nostrils expanding trying to catch some of their poisoned air. By the time I got to the station I would convince myself that if I had just one cigarette it would sort me out for the rest of the day. So I would find the nearest smoker, make some useless joke about giving up smoking, and then beg for a cigarette. I would smoke it, then go and sit with all my fellow non-smokers in the non-smoking carriage. You have to remember that it was not that long ago that you could smoke on trains, on buses, in cinemas and in the office at work.

On arrival at work (I worked in a bank for a few years) I would be hit with a wall of cigarette smoke as I entered the main banking hall. You were allowed to smoke until 9.30 a.m., then the bank opened to the public and all smoking was reserved for the toilets and the staffroom. Looking back, it must have been horrible for the non-smokers to have to come and eat their lunch in the staffroom where at least 20 to 30 people smoked. Anyway, if I could get to 9.30 a.m. without a smoke there was always a sense of achievement, obviously not counting the cigarette at the station – that was for medicinal reasons. As long as I had a good morning, there was a chance I could get to noon. Even so, I would have worked out whom I had not recently scrounged a cigarette from so there would be somebody willing to donate one if I became desperate. By the time I went to lunch (avoiding the staffroom) I would concentrate on walking in a smoke-free environment, which normally meant somewhere down by the river. Nine times out of ten I would not last the whole walk; I would pass a shop, buy a pack of ten, smoke one, swear at myself and then throw the rest in the bin. At the same time I would give myself a stiff talking to and resolve that whatever happened I would never smoke again. On days like those when I was trying to give up, you would find me in the evening in the pub with a pack of Marlboro and five pints. My comments to anyone asking me if I was giving up would be, 'If you are going to smoke you might as well enjoy it'. In reality, I had to limit my giving-up days to no more than three a week, as I was in danger of becoming an alcoholic.

I would not describe myself as a completely weak-willed person, as I've always done what I've wanted in life, including travelling and surfing all around the world. I now teach martial arts and Pilates as part of earning my living, and work in physiotherapy clinics in Kent using rehabilitation exercises to get people active and mobile. I raced motorcycles for ten years – winning (and crashing) in many events. Part of my work involves standing in front of large groups of people, teaching and lecturing on various life skills. I would have always described myself as an active, sporty person; however, when it came to smoking I used to feel like a slave – a weak pathetic fool who, although he sometimes hated smoking, could not stop. I would convince myself that obviously some people are smokers, some are not, and those who are not just don't know what they are missing. How wrong I was! Everyone could become a smoker if they were not aware of the nicotine trap and if they were coaxed into trying it for long enough.

When you appreciate that all the positives about smoking and the reasons for doing it are simply excuses and unreal, then it is hard to understand why you did not realize that in the first place. If you had been given this information before you smoked your first cigarette then you would never have started at all.

The aim of this book is obvious – to persuade you to stop smoking. The way in which it works is to demonstrate that all the supposed reasons as to why you want or need to smoke are false, and to show the real benefits enjoyed by those who do not smoke.

How to use this book

The best way to use this book is to read a chapter or two at a time. If you were to read the book in one go that would not allow enough time for your brain to digest the information and arguments it contains. I come across many people who have read quickly through books on how to stop smoking. They can spout most of the points, but they are only paying lip service, and their comments are often accompanied by an 'and I will get round to stopping smoking next month when I can focus on it'.

Skipping through is not enough. As a reader of this book you have an important job to perform. Your job is to question what you are reading and to make decisions on what you want in your future. By reading this book a bit at a time, your brain will come to its own conclusions. Once everything is clear to you, you will have the answers to the basic question that all smokers ask themselves: 'How can I stop smoking?'

Key points and solutions are highlighted throughout the book; most of them are in boxes at the end of the chapters or within the chapters. I have listed at the back of the book the 50 key points that will help to keep you smoke free, but please feel free to highlight or write down your own on the blank pages at the end of the book. Some may apply more to your situation than others, but it is important that you understand them all fully. You may be persuaded to give up smoking after reading a few pages, but please continue through to the end so that every angle and eventuality has been covered and you really do stop for good! Don't worry. There is no chanting of mantras or wailing while you beat yourself with rosary beads. This book is based on facts and basic truths about why we smoke, and provides conclusive answers as to why and how you can stop.

When to read this book

The best time to read this book is when you are taking a five- or ten-minute break. Indeed, most of the chapters are designed to be read while having a smoke. That is when you are likely to be at your calmest. Whatever I say in this book is not going to worry you. If you feel uncomfortable you can always light up another cigarette. The other useful reason for reading while you are smoking is that you normally think about smoking when you are not doing it. There is no need to think about smoking while you are doing it. Why would you? When you are smoking you are relieving the problem of needing a smoke. By thinking about smoking while doing it, you will actually look forward to not smoking rather than the other way round. Let me say that again: 'Very soon you will look forward to the times when you are not smoking and soon after that you will look forward to the time when you never have to or want to smoke again.' Most smokers want to stop. They know that they should not do it, but they think that they need to or enjoy smoking and cannot see their lives without it.

Don't worry

Many smokers fear that, even though they might be able to stop smoking, they will then spend the rest of their lives continuing to crave for something they cannot have. It's not going to be like that. By the end of this book you will understand how you became a smoker and what smoking has done for you. You will understand that you never really wanted to be a smoker. In reality, you were fooled into smoking without realizing the trick that was being played on you. After all, what is the worst that can happen? The worst is that you could still be smoking and you would end the experience with a book that is perfect for wedging the door open on hot, windy days. By reading this book you have everything to gain and nothing to lose.

Who should read this book?

This might seem like a stupid question but this book is not just intended for people who smoke. If you have given up smoking by other means and you still miss the experience, then this book is going to be very useful to you. If you are a concerned parent worried about your children smoking, then this book will help you to understand what you are up against. Chapter 15 covers children and smoking. Chapter 22, 'Young smokers', is a condensed version of some of the other chapters. This chapter takes only 10–15 minutes to read and is designed to encourage young people to read the whole book. Encouraging children and young people to understand the nature and dangers of smoking is essential. Adult smokers are the biggest enemy of young smokers. Parental and other adult example is crucial. If you smoke, then your children or other children with whom you come into contact are likely to smoke. They are copying you and they have you as an excuse.

Most people who read this book will be adults. Remember, as an adult you can choose to do what you want to do. This book will tell you what is actually going on in your world of smoking. You will soon find out that the only people who are making you do something that you do not want to do are the people who make cigarettes. Nothing is going to be taken away from you and you will not feel deprived. In fact, you are going to get more out of yourself by doing less.

Knowing where you are and where you need to get to

Imagine you have never driven a car before but someone puts you in the driver's seat and gives you the key. You have not got a clue; you do not know where the key goes, which pedal does what or how to take the handbrake off. You do not even know how to get started, let alone pull away; you realize that something is not right but you do not see it as your responsibility. You are in a state of unconscious incompetence. You do not even know where you are going so there seems little point to try.

Then someone gives you a map, tells you what the car does, shows you how to start it and explains that your aim is to get the car from A to B. You play with the controls and sometimes you get it right and the car moves, but you cannot even make it out of the car park. You are still not going anywhere because you do not know how to use the controls properly.

You feel uneasy because you want to get to place B; you realize something needs to happen but you are still incapable of moving forward. You are in a state of conscious incompetence. You realize there is a problem but any movement forwards is pure luck rather than by design.

Then someone patiently shows you how everything works and the rules of the road. So if you concentrate and stay focused you can carefully proceed to point B. You are now in a state of conscious competence. If you consciously make an effort you can get to where you want to go. You have to concentrate and tell yourself what to do before you do it, but as long as you stay alert you can easily and safely arrive at your destination. After some months of practice you can get in your car and, without thinking about it, you find driving it takes no thought at all. You are in a state of unconscious competence. You don't have to remind yourself of 'mirror, signal, manoeuvre' or think about which pedal or button does what. The only time you have to concentrate hard is when you are going somewhere different or driving in adverse conditions.

As a smoker who knows that they want to stop, you are generally in a state of conscious incompetence that sometimes dips into conscious competence. So when you are very focused and concentrating you can control smoking but it seems such an effort that you keep ending up back in the same place because no one has given you a map and a plan of how to get there. When you get frustrated, your mood tells you where to go – back to smoking. It feels safer and you tell yourself you will try harder when you feel better. It's as if you have just driven to the outer limits of the city, but instead of venturing on into a new adventure you do what you always do and turn back to the safety of home. The problem is that you are relying on your mood rather than a plan. You are relying on your feelings instead of action.

Key point

If you rely on your mood, you are screwed.

By the end of this book you will be in a state of conscious competence/unconscious competence. As time goes on, it will become more and more unconscious; the only time you will have to think about it is when you are in vulnerable or different surroundings. In the beginning it makes sense to limit awkward situations that will trip you up and to look out for potential potholes so you can avoid them. This book is a map, and with a little planning it will be easy to get you nicotine-free and content never to have to smoke again.

1

We already know we shouldn't smoke

We all know that we should not smoke. We all know that smoking is bad for you. As smokers, we all know that we should stop smoking and we have all used some form of excuse to ourselves and to our friends to justify the fact that we still do it. Some of the excuses do not sound too ludicrous and some are even funny, but we all know that they are not true.

- If it were not for the tax revenue from smoking, the government would not be able to run the National Health Service.

- No one has ever proved that smoking is bad for you.

- My grandmother smoked constantly and she lived until she was 92 years old.

- I hear that the lungs of a smoker are stronger than those of a non-smoker because they have had to work harder. I consider myself in training when I am smoking.

- I know it's not good for me but I will give up by the time I am 30, or maybe when I am 40.

- Smoking is one of the few things in life I enjoy. If I had to give it up, what pleasures would I have left?

- If you stop smoking, stop drinking, stop having sex and stop taking drugs they say you will live longer. It only seems longer.

- Smoking really calms my nerves. I always feel much better after a cigarette.

- So I'm a nicotine addict; at least I am not a drug addict.

- When I get pregnant, I will definitely stop smoking.

- If I did not have my own brand of cigarette I would not bother smoking. I really enjoy the taste of it.

- With a cup of coffee there is nothing better than a good smoke.

- I only smoke when I drink.

- My husband only smokes in the evening.

- I'm only a social smoker; I never buy my own.

- It's something to do with my hands.

- If I have a cup of tea and a smoke it stops me eating.

These are just excuses. We cannot say to our non-smoking friends and family what we think is the truth. Which is that we are not in control of our lives and this little pack of weed makes our life complete, so that without it we cannot be useful or happy and to give up would only make us miserable. We have tried on many occasions, and even though we know that smoking is bad for us in every way, we will be happier smoking than not smoking. If we tried to explain that to our non-smoking friends they would look at us strangely. We would probably be nervous of their replies. We might worry that they would always pity us in some demeaning way. Well, you wouldn't be far wrong. Try to see it from their point of view as non-smokers.

They see you hurting yourself, throwing your money away, complaining that you can't live without it and wishing at the same time that you'd never started. As non-smokers they wonder why you ever wanted to start in the first place. They relay to you some story about when they had tried to smoke a cigarette but it tasted so awful that they threw it away and never went near one again. You must remember that even the most fervent anti-smoker could still become a nicotine addict. Just find a way of hiding nicotine in something they like eating and once they get that little mental craving into their system you could introduce smoking and then they would want it, without totally understanding why.

For over 20 years my mother had been telling me that I was a nicotine addict. My reply to her was that I could give up if I wanted but it was something that I enjoyed. Whenever I was having a conversation with her and I was getting a bit moody, she would wind me up and tell me that I was getting my withdrawal symptoms again and should pop out and have a cigarette before we carried on our conversation. I would point out to her that if I wanted a cigarette I would have one and that she should not change the conversation just because she did not agree with what I had to say. At this point I would normally accuse her of not listening, and storm out and go for a smoke. While smoking my cigarette I would mutter to myself how my mother did not understand me, and by the end of my cigarette I would feel calmer. I would then return to the discussion with my mother, pointing out that I had chosen to smoke and the reason I was now more reasonable was that I had got away from her for five minutes.

In her day, my mother was a well-respected nurse and she has cared for many people, including those with addictive problems. In her view, as far as the destruction of people's bodies was concerned, she saw little difference between the addiction to strong drugs, alcohol or cigarettes. She would try to frighten me with stories of people having their legs amputated due to clogged arteries from smoking, or having to speak through a box in their neck because of throat cancer. You would have thought that with an anti-smoking nurse for a mother the message would have been clear; the problem was that I did not totally understand the nature of addiction. I certainly did not believe that in a civilized world we could actually allow companies to mass-produce a product whose only effect was to kill people early, making those companies rich and keeping the National Health Service overworked.

When I was 18, my mother and I sat with my grandfather as he breathed his last few breaths in a small hospital in Surrey. Dying from emphysema means slowly losing lung capacity, and so experiencing increasingly severe breathing difficulties. Knowing that my grandfather had been a heavy smoker and his illness was completely smoking-related, you'd have thought that I would have given up for good, there and then. After my grandfather died, I smoked over 20 cigarettes in one evening. The first one was standing outside the hospital within ten minutes of his death. My grandmother is still alive today in her nineties and maybe if my grandfather had not smoked he might still be around. It's a pity that for the sake of sucking on a bit of weed, millions of people's lives will be cut short for absolutely no benefit.

Luckily, smoking is relatively easy to stop because the addiction is very mild and can be completely controlled by your mind. In contrast, coming off alcohol or a heavy heroin addiction has much more intense mental and even fatal physical risks. My mother would get angry that people were not properly educated about the nature of these addictive substances. Personally, I was quite a stubborn kid. No one could tell me anything, and like many young people, I had to learn things for myself – sometimes the easy way, sometimes the hard way. Even though my mother had been telling me for 22 years that smoking was an addictive, filthy waste of time, it took until I was in my thirties before it really hit me.

I was watching a comedian go through his routine and he was doing a piece on his relationship with his girlfriend. In this sketch his girlfriend was not coming round to sleep with him as much as she used to do; he was so worried that his girlfriend was going to leave him that he had started putting nicotine patches on her while she was sleeping. He would then carefully peel them off just before she woke. After a week she was in his bed every night, complaining of an uneasy feeling whenever she was not with him. The relationship was a success until two weeks later she took up smoking and left him. On hearing that I laughed (his delivery was better than mine) and then quite

seriously thought: would that work? After thinking about it all night I came to a conclusion that made it easy to stop smoking! I stopped soon after that day and have never wanted or had another cigarette since.

For me, not smoking was a pleasurable thing. Every day without smoking became more enjoyable than the last. Even though I am not a religious man, when I first stopped smoking I would see other people smoking and thank God that I did not have to do that anymore. Even though the reason for not needing to smoke is the same as the reason for needing to (i.e. nicotine), the answer or answers that you come up with as to why you will never want to smoke may be different from mine. Near the end of the book, once we have discussed all the reasons why you thought that you wanted to smoke, you will have your own list of positive answers which explain why smoking is something you will never want to do again even if someone paid you. All the smokers who have successfully stopped that I have talked to have a slightly different list of answers, but with the same basic theme. When I say 'successfully' stopped, I mean people who have stopped smoking, not those who have given up but still miss it. When you have all the answers clear in your head, then you realize that there is nothing to miss. Even if you are a confident person, the new-found freedom that comes from not smoking will be enjoyable and give you a sense of optimism for your future as a non-smoker.

Solution 1

When you get to the point of realizing you never want to smoke again, you almost want to bottle the sensation, it is such a pleasurable feeling.

2

One day soon

One day soon, if not already, you will realize that time is the most precious thing you have. Whatever you choose to spend your time doing – being with friends and family, travelling, participating in sport, working or providing for others – is up to you. If you are young, then getting old or ill seems like a lifetime away, but if you look around on the street at people much older than you, you begin to realize that it happens to us all. Obviously, we are all going to die at some point; that's inevitable. We should not be afraid of dying, but we should be afraid of not living our lives the way we want to. As smokers, we are not in control of part of our lives, as we are addicts or almost slaves to its addiction. Smoking wastes our lives and takes us away from spending time getting on with what we want to do.

This is not just physically but also mentally. As a person that wants to stop smoking, think about how many times a day smoking enters your head and how much you have to fit your life around it. How many times have you left the house forgetting your keys, an umbrella, your wallet, a phone or to post a letter? I bet you rarely forget to pick up your cigarettes or pipe. If you are running low, you make sure you have enough cash and time to stop off and pick up a fresh pack.

You never made a conscious, rational decision to start smoking. If you can actually remember the first time you had a cigarette, that experience would have involved you coughing and feeling unwell. Especially if you smoked the whole cigarette and took it all down, rather than just swilling the smoke around your mouth and blowing it out. The frightening fact is that everyone could become a smoker if they were fooled into trying it. Luckily, in the western world, there are tight controls on smoking and it is viewed as being more unpopular than ever before, but that is still not enough.

Smokers are the worst advertisements for smoking. Intelligent, bright, literate, sensible individuals like you. There is no way that you would go up to people in the street or even friends and start telling them that they are missing out on a great opportunity by not smoking. However, if people have not already made the decision not to smoke, there is still a chance that they may be tempted to take it up. What would your advice be to them?

Young people see you smoking and think, 'Well if that person smokes it can't be such a bad thing to do or they would not do it', or 'Surely they enjoy it or they would not do it. There must be some pleasure in smoking because otherwise why do so many parents and adults do it?' What would your advice be to a 12-year-old who was thinking of starting smoking?

Even if you are the most ardent pro-smoker, your answer would be the same as any non-smoker. Do not start smoking! This answer proves that every smoker would like to stop if they could. As smokers we often wonder why we ever started, we give ourselves reasons and excuses why we still smoke or keep failing to quit.

Once you fully understand the nature of smoking and all the false myths and excuses around why you think you smoke, then there becomes no need or desire to smoke. This will happen some day soon and as a non-smoker you will look back at all the fuss and wonder why you ever smoked. You will never forget that enjoyable feeling of being free from the weed. Once you understand all the false reasons why you smoked, it will be easy never to want to smoke again. Smoking is the unwanted guest at a party. You never meant to invite him but now he is here, you cannot get rid of him. If you could say the right thing or make him feel unwelcome then he would leave, but it just never seems like the right time.

At some point in our smoking lives, we must have felt that we enjoyed smoking or we would not have done it. If you enjoy something it means you like doing it, but you do not have to do it all the time. I personally enjoy surfing, going for walks, spending time with my family and kissing my wife. I would not want to spend my whole time doing just one of those things so I choose the time when I enjoy these favourite pastimes. Take something like chocolate – a favourite foodstuff for most of us (or some other food if you prefer). I bet that with the smallest amount of willpower you could stay off it for a whole week. You could even place it on your desk at work and, in spite of it being in your face all day, you could easily avoid eating it. After a while you would not even notice the bar of chocolate and you might even forget it was there.

Now try the same with a pack of cigarettes and try not to have one for a week. By halfway through the first day you will imagine the pack is talking to you. It will be saying to you things like, 'Go on, just have the one, it won't hurt to have just one; you deserve it; you have resisted me for all that time, pat yourself on the back and go and enjoy having a smoke, I won't tell.' Later on that day you will start having a conversation with a pack of cigarettes and think you are going mad. That little voice is the part of your brain that needs its fix of nicotine. For some people it helps to imagine that voice as an evil villain or a little monster. In the first couple of weeks when you stop smoking, visualize destroying that little monster each time it tells you to smoke. The thing that keeps telling you to smoke is your nicotine brain; a part of your brain that feeds and craves its little fix. As it gets fed less and less nicotine, it will starve and die and the craving for nicotine will disappear.

How you spend your time should be up to you and the choices you make should be within your control. Smoking is not under your complete control. It controls you; it tells you when it is time to have another smoke. Whether you do so or not is up to you, depending on the situation or whether you have the willpower to resist. But unless you're aware of the subtle trappings of smoking and understand why you do it, sooner or later you will succumb to having a cigarette.

There are many people who still want to have a cigarette, but as a result of extreme willpower are not allowing themselves what they think is a great pleasure. I have come across people that still crave a cigarette even after ten years of not having one because they still think that it is pleasurable. Or people who have not smoked for five years and have gone back to smoking only to wonder what all the fuss was about and to stop smoking again a week later. Once you have worked out for yourself that you are no longer a smoker, it will be easy never to have that desire. Even though stopping smoking has a very slight physical withdrawal effect, the main enemy is your mind.

Your mind has been conditioned to believe that smoking gives you some sort of relief or tiny high, and that without it you feel insecure and unfulfilled. This sensation of fear or loss is the mental prison within which smoking holds you. Once your brain has all the answers to dealing with that fear, the fear will no longer exist. Like a child who is afraid of the dark because they have seen too many scary movies or been told frightening stories, once they realize that those imaginary monsters in the wardrobe do not exist they can happily go to sleep unafraid of the dark. Once your mind realizes it is being conned by smoking, it becomes easy and enjoyable to stop.

Stopping smoking not only means losing a sense of fear, it also produces obvious benefits for your health, well-being and state of mind. As you read through this book, all the reasons why you think you smoke become the obvious answers to why you should *not* smoke. The same basic plot runs throughout this book, as you would expect. You do not want to smoke and you never wanted to. Remember you never chose to be a smoker, smoking chose you; just like no one chooses to be an alcoholic or a crack addict. Smoking wastes your life and takes much away from you but gives no reward. You have everything to gain and nothing to lose by stopping smoking.

Solution 2

You should be the one making the choices in your life, not some unrewarding drug that costs you an arm and possibly a leg.

3

Welcome back to your senses

One of the great pleasures of stopping smoking is that life will taste better in every way. You will notice that your sense of smell improves dramatically, along with your taste. You will also notice how much you used to stink. Even when you stand next to a smoker who is not smoking, you can't help but say to yourself, 'Did I really smell that bad?' When I think back to my youth, I cannot remember many of the girls that I went out with who did not smoke. Most of the relationships I had with non-smokers did not last very long and it's easy to see why. I am sure it had nothing to do with my charming sense of humour and laid-back, nearly horizontal attitude to life (lazy, cheeky and teller of bad jokes).

Even after as little as a week you will not fail to notice the pleasant aromas your nasal passages are picking up. However, by far the biggest improvement will be in the taste of your food. Some people worry about putting on a few pounds when they give up smoking, but the only real reason why this might happen is that the foodstuffs you have been eating will suddenly taste a whole lot better. It's as if you've had a cold for the past ten years and now it's gone.

By stopping smoking you will also benefit from a great sense of achievement. You will have freed yourself from many years of mental slavery; freed yourself from that sense of fear that followed you whenever you were without a cigarette. Think about it! You actually thought you enjoyed smoking. As a smoker, if I told you that you could not have a cigarette for three days, how would you feel after three hours, let alone three days? You would feel anxious, agitated and moody; none of those is a pleasurable sensation. The great deal is that when you stop smoking those sensations soon disappear and each day is better than the last, until one day you ask 'What was all the fuss about?' Obviously, you have to be a little bit careful when you say this, as when everything is obvious and clear in your head you cannot go back to being a nicotine addict. This means you cannot ever put a cigarette in your mouth again.

With that sense of anxiety that lingers around you as a smoker, comes the obvious fear for your health and that frightening question of 'Will this next cigarette be the one to trigger off the fatal disease that will kill me?' There's a very real chance that this *is* going to happen. As smokers, we all think it will not happen to us and we will be the one to buck the trend. I really wish it were so for every one of those people that decides to carry on smoking, but it is not. Just living with that fear should be enough to make you stop. Unfortunately, the clever trap of nicotine is so cunningly subtle that we are fooled into believing otherwise.

One of the ladies who comes to my Tai Chi classes has had many discussions with me about smoking. Until recently, she smoked somewhere between 25 and 30 cigarettes a day. She comes to see me for Tai Chi, not because she wants to stop smoking, so unless she brings it up I leave it at that. Nevertheless, she has pointed out to me that she only smokes one particular brand, can afford it and thinks that the health issues around smoking are greatly exaggerated. Until she sees absolute proof of the downsides of smoking, she is going to enjoy every last cigarette. My answer to that would be, 'Good for you. It is important to enjoy what you do as long as you do enjoy it'. This particular lady is in her early fifties, elegant, attractive, fit and regularly attends the gym. Recently she has been having blackouts. Whether these are connected with smoking or not, I cannot say, but the important thing is she believes it to be the case, so she has cut down. She has reduced to six a day, only smoking the cigarettes that she feels are the ones she enjoys. If I decided to discuss this with her, she would still defend her enjoyment of smoking and say, 'C'est la vie'.

When she smoked 25 a day, she didn't notice her craving for nicotine because she was satisfying it 'on demand'. Now that she rations herself to six a day, she is counting every precious cigarette that she smokes and suffering those annoying cravings every day of her life. We are all born with an inherent sense of optimism and self-preservation. If not, why would we bother getting out of bed every morning? For me the mental anguish that this situation creates would be more destructive than the six cigarettes. As we all know, mental attitude has an enormous effect on our physical well-being. So not only are we being tortured physically but mentally too.

Imagine that you are still in the prime of your life but now the warning bells are starting to go off. You have been getting away with it for so long but now your body is at a crossroads where every cigarette you smoke is going to produce a marked deterioration in your health. Every day you get out of bed and you spend some of that morning thinking how long you can go before that first cigarette out of your six. How could you just smoke the cigarettes that you enjoy? You do not enjoy *any* of them! Instead of enjoying the rest of your life, you are making your coffin, and every cigarette you smoke is another nail banged into it.

Whether you realize it yet or not, as a smoker you have no control over your smoking, whether you smoke one or 100 a day. At least if you smoke 100 a day that fear and the pain of smoking should not last too long!

When you stop smoking you regain control of many of your senses and a part of your mind. Think about it: you no longer have to worry about where you are and when you can slip in your next fix. You can take your time with your meal and really enjoy the aromas and flavours that the food has to offer, rather than bolting it down and grabbing the nearest ashtray, or popping outside while you leave everyone in the room to enjoy their meal. You won't have to look at the clock again and plan your next break, or sneak off to the toilet for a quick cigarette when no one's looking. You will be able to concentrate on the task in hand without having the nagging sensation that you should be lighting up.

Smoking is like any vicious circle. The more you do it, the more you want it, but the more it destroys your senses and your well-being. As soon as you stop, the circle changes from a vicious one to a virtuous one. I do not mean that you sprout wings, save little dogs from drowning, stop swearing and sing *The Sound Of Music* wherever you go. I mean that the positive action of stopping smoking will have a knock-on effect on your general attitude and outlook on life. As a smoker, you know you are harming yourself with absolutely no gain. When you stop, you will naturally have improved confidence about your abilities to control your life and what is achievable. It is as if

you have stepped out from under a grey cloud that has been parked over your head for many years. If you do not believe me, ask an ex-smoker. You probably will not want to, as, to smokers, there is nothing much worse than listening to the self-righteous, positive, confident, enlightened ex-smoker. But as you will soon find out, the reason they go on so much is because it feels, and it *is*, great not to smoke.

The gains of stopping smoking are so great that at this point I almost feel like advising people to take up smoking for a short while in order to enjoy all the wonderful sensations of giving up. Then even more people could wander around with a smug look on their faces, especially when they see somebody smoking. I will not say it, though, because it would be irresponsible and my publisher would certainly not approve. If you do stump up the confidence to listen to the almost pious sermon you will receive from an ex-smoker, make sure you speak to somebody who really has stopped and who understands why, not to someone who is simply relying on willpower. For, as I have already suggested, people who rely on willpower alone may still miss smoking. In contrast, the message of this book is that when you can honestly answer all the questions in your mind as to why you smoke, there will be no reason to do so. You will stop, and you will not miss it.

Solution 3

Smoking is literally like a cloud obscuring your senses; once you stop, you can enjoy the clarity of life you deserve.

4

Nicotine

Nicotine is a substance found in the tobacco plant. It is the substance you crave every time you feel the need for a cigarette. Nicotine is a powerful toxin. If you were to ingest only 60mg of it in its pure form, you would be dead within minutes. A typical cigarette contains 8mg of nicotine and will deliver somewhere between 0.5mg to 2mg of nicotine to the smoker, depending on how hard you suck or how much you cover up the ventilation holes on the filter. The drug travels to the brain within eight seconds when smoked, which is much quicker than if you chew it, inject it or put a nicotine patch on your skin. That's why, when you have that craving for nicotine, you feel a quick sense of relief as soon as you start sucking down that smoke. That's why in your mind you always regard smoking as a pleasurable experience, even when you know you do not want to do it. Nicotine triggers several neurotransmitters in the brain, causing the release of other substances called noradrenaline and dopamine – these act as stimulants on the body.

Noradrenaline works by stimulating receptors around the body. This narrows the blood vessels in the extremities and redirects blood to the essential organs, such as the heart, increasing blood pressure and preparing the body for action. This is why many smokers when they stop smoking lose the sense of fear and anxiety which is caused by smoking.

Anyone who recalls their basic biology classes will remember the 'fight or flight' response, which is created when your body produces adrenaline. This makes the body direct blood to the essential organs because you are in a situation in which you are either going to have to run away or get involved in a fight. What normally creates adrenaline in our bodies is a healthy amount of fear, which in the right situation is not a bad thing.

During the Second World War it was thought to be a good idea to give free cigarettes to soldiers to increase their confidence but, if you think about it, smoking actually increases fear and insecurity because it releases noradrenaline. Unfortunately, unless the soldiers smoked constantly, this possibly had the reverse effect. (Of course if they did smoke constantly it would have impaired their ability to run up hills or take aim with a weapon. It might even have killed them before the enemy got the chance.)

Dopamine is a neurotransmitter that acts as a mood enhancer and a stimulant; it can be used to improve the movements of Parkinson's sufferers. Dopamine could be described as the happy drug of the brain. This might suggest an argument for the benefits of smoking! Unfortunately, as a smoker, you soon build up your immunity to nicotine and the effects it has on you. As your brain builds up more receptors to the drug, it requires more of the drug just to maintain a level state. This means that unless you increase your nicotine intake you will find it difficult to maintain a level feeling of happiness, as your brain needs more of the drug. Therefore, after a while, all you're doing when smoking is trying to return to the peaceful sense of balance in your brain you had before you ever started smoking. Even today, with our ability to create almost anything, you would be hard pressed to come up with such a subtle and addictive drug. Besides, although the release of dopamine can be associated with a sense of euphoria, its long-term use has some negative side-effects. The following is just a partial list of the possible side-effects of dopamine:

▶ headache

▶ chest pain

▶ low blood pressure

▶ palpitations

▶ difficulty in breathing

▶ irregular heart beats

▶ reduced blood flow to the extremities

▶ dilated pupils

▶ mental health problems.

So with the release of these drugs into your body there is a hit to be had from smoking a cigarette. But for a smoker really to notice it, they would have to smoke just one week out of 52. Hands up if you know any smoker who can do that!

The problem with having one or a few cigarettes is that you end up wanting the other thousand that come with it. All you are doing as a smoker is trying to get back to that calm state of mind that a non-smoker feels. The great thing is, though, that when you understand the nature of the beast and its hold on you, it becomes easy to conquer it.

Solution 4

Nicotine is not a drug you take by choice; it is a clever substance that perpetuates your need for it.

5

What's in your daily smoke?

Marlboro is the world's bestselling cigarette brand. It is owned by the largest tobacco company, Philip Morris USA, which is part of the Altria group. In the 1960s it was much less significant as a tobacco company and was ranked only sixth largest in the world. Then something shifted; the clever scientists at the Philip Morris laboratories changed how they made their cigarettes. Over the next decade they became the leading company in cigarette sales, with Marlboro accounting for one in every five cigarettes sold. This does not even include the other top-selling brands also made by Philip Morris.

The company argued that it was its marketing strategy, which included the incarnation of the 'Marlboro Man' and 'Welcome to Marlboro Country', which helped it to shift these extra thousand billion cigarettes. The other leading tobacco companies knew that this was not the reason, and their scientific researchers started reverse engineering Marlboro cigarettes to find out what made them so desirable. They found that Marlboro was using ammoniated sheet material in the manufacture of its cigarettes. This ammonia in the burning cigarette increased the alkalinity of the smoke entering the smoker. This in turn increased the dose of nicotine absorption into the bloodstream of any smoker, giving a more effective relief from the withdrawal symptoms of nicotine.

The other clever aspect of the newly designed Marlboro cigarettes was that, when tested, they showed reduced tar levels, even though each cigarette was delivering a bigger nicotine hit! This tar reduction was used in Marlboro advertising to promote the new cigarette as a healthier smoke. In fact the reverse was true. By increasing the density of nicotine gas in the smoke, the new cigarettes were able to evade the standard measuring process that tests for the amount of tar residue left on the filter when smoked. Very clever.

It didn't stop there. Once other tobacco companies found out that they could increase the nicotine content and still manage to slip under government health restrictions, they all did it. At present, there are over 500 additives used in the production of cigarettes. Some additives, such as cocoa, honey, liquorice, sugar and vanilla, sound quite harmless, and tobacco companies would argue that many of the additives in a cigarette are there simply to enhance the flavour and smooth taste of the smoke.

Just a thought . . . if the companies' claims are true, ask yourself what is the difference between putting nicotine into children's sweets such as chocolate or sugary cereals, and putting those same sweet flavours into a cigarette. I would guess the answer would be billions of pounds profit or a lengthy prison sentence for trying to poison people. My point is that legislation covering the production of tobacco is lax in comparison with the very tight guidelines on what goes into the products we eat. However, here is an interesting question: if companies could get away with putting nicotine in food products to make them addictive, would they do it? I'll let you answer that.

In 1989 there was an interesting incident concerning a million cases of imported fruit. The fruit was banned from entering the country after a small amount of cyanide was found in just two grapes. There is 33 times more cyanide in one single cigarette than was found in those two grapes.

Other 'less harmful' products found in some brands of cigarettes are eugenol (the main component in the essential oil extracted from cloves) and menthol. I only ever smoked menthol cigarettes for three reasons.

- I thought it made me smell more minty; so that if I was going to be in close proximity to my mother soon after smoking, she would not smell the smoke on my breath.

- There was nothing better being offered to me at school break-time.

- If I had a sore throat or a congested chest, it would be less painful to get my fix from a menthol cigarette.

When I was younger I considered menthol cigarettes to be the healthier smoke as they seemed to have a soft sensation on the throat and you could comfortably smoke more of them. In my mind, menthol cigarettes were not so bad for you. What I did not realize back then was that the menthol sensation in the smoke would slightly numb the throat to reduce the irritating effect.

It had nothing to do with being a cooler, milder smoke at all. I remember having to suck harder on mentholated cigarettes, even harder when I did not have a sore throat, just to make sure some smoke was going down.

Some would argue that those sweet-flavoured additives like cocoa and honey make cigarettes tastier to all age groups – children and adults. Some of those additives are used to take away the harshness and the irritant effect. But the biggest reason for including additives such as liquorice, sugar, organic acids and salt is that they enhance the receptiveness of the smoker to nicotine, in a similar way to the inhalers used by asthma sufferers; inhalers are designed to deliver their drug as efficiently as possible. Those 'gentle' ingredients in your cigarette are designed to give maximum nicotine dispersal throughout your lungs and into your bloodstream.

It took a lot of men in white coats and an immense number of nicotine-crazed rats and other lab animals to establish these findings. Those people and creatures are still hard at work while you are reading this book, and it is all for your benefit.

When all these different ingredients burn together, they obviously create smoke. This smoke is made up of sidestream and mainstream smoke. Mainstream is the smoke you get from the filter or mouth end of the cigarette, and sidestream is that which comes from the burning end of the cigarette. Many of the toxins are found in higher concentrations in sidestream smoke than in the mainstream. Before smoking was banned in public places, in the average smoky pub or bar up to 85 per cent of the smoke could be from sidestream. You don't need a scientist or a lab technician to tell you that this smoke is poisonous to our bodies; just find someone with only a slightly sensitive breathing condition, let alone an asthma sufferer, and take them into a smoke-filled room and watch them choke. Indeed, since most of this smoke is coming from the lit end of the cigarette, you could argue that the safest place to be is at the other end, where the filter is. But at least someone who does not smoke is free to leave that smoked-filled area, whereas as a smoker you have to take it with you. We shall talk more about the real effects of secondary smoke in a later chapter.

TRUST US, WE ARE THE TOBACCO COMPANY

So without getting too technical, here are some of the chemicals found in the smoke of a cigarette.

- ▶ Carbon monoxide – yes, the same stuff that you would get if you sucked on the exhaust fumes of a car.

- ▶ Naphthalene – derived from coal tar and best-known for its use in the making of mothballs.

- ▶ Arsenic – which, among other things, is used as an insecticide to kill ants.

- ▶ Cyanide – yes, a component of the gas used in the Nazi gas chambers.

- ▶ Phenol – next time you clean your toilet, you will probably be using this substance.

- ▶ Ammonia – this is used in products such as fertilizer and floor cleaner.

These are just some of the harmful chemicals that you are putting into your body when you light up. Many of these substances are carcinogenic – they greatly increase the risk of cancer. But you probably already knew that.

Did you realize, however, that many of these substances are put into a cigarette just to make you more addicted to nicotine and to mask the roughness and irritant effect of smoking undiluted nicotine? As the tobacco companies admit, cigarettes are a tool for the delivery of nicotine into the human body. So tobacco companies will do anything they can to improve that delivery and maintain your addiction.

Does it seem wrong to you, as it does to me, that these companies view their customers as an expendable financial crop that can be herded and financially fleeced without actually realizing it? It makes me angry, but you can do something about it, as I did. By the end of this book, when you stop smoking and stop buying cigarettes, you will be taking away some of their income and some of their power, while bringing the control and power back to yourself.

Solution 5

To regain control, you need to realize that the tobacco companies have been controlling you.

6

Choice

I was having a discussion with a friend recently while driving to Brighton. I enjoy the arguments we have, although they sometimes become quite heated. We both learn something new and we are still good friends afterwards, even though we often shout at each other. His argument was that people should be allowed to do what they want when it comes to their own bodies. His point was that if he wanted to smoke heroin, he should be allowed to, and the government should make all drugs legal so they could tax them and make a tidy profit and ensure stricter controls. My view was that with so many more people desperate for a fix, every penny taken in tax and a lot more money besides would be spent dealing with the millions of people in rehab and the amount of crime. In addition, if drugs like cocaine were made legal, it would be much easier for younger people to come into contact with them, and they would be heavily targeted by dealers and suppliers.

My friend argued that, if they were made legal, the quality of drugs would become superior and there would be fewer problems. I agreed with the first point, but not the second. You might have people outside schools selling drugs mixed in with sherbet dips and liquorice allsorts. If big business got involved, you might even end up with most of the world addicted to heroin and a larger health problem than obesity, heart disease and smoking-related illnesses put together. At present, there are about 10 million smokers in the UK – about 21 per cent of men and 20 per cent of women in the total population. With the ban on tobacco advertising and a better understanding of the health consequences of smoking, these percentages are much lower than in the early 1970s, when nearly half the population – 51 per cent of men and 41 per cent of women – smoked.

Nicotine is cleverly addictive; both the effects and withdrawal sensations are subtle and irritating, unlike the withdrawal symptoms from a drug like heroin: cold sweats, violent behaviour, a sensation that your body is going to explode as your heart pounds louder and louder, convulsions, diarrhoea, insomnia and, in more frail people, heart attacks and death. The worst physical effect when you stop smoking is a slight irritation, which is less irksome than a runny nose.

I explained these points to my friend and then pointed out that he had not even managed to stop smoking yet, and to think how much harder it would be for him, an intelligent and educated person, to kick the heroin addiction in comparison to the nicotine addiction. I thought it was reckless to suppose that people, especially children, could handle such freedom of choice – when all the consequences and risks are not appreciated and the aims of the people supplying the drug (solely to make money) are not understood. His reply was that he had chosen to smoke because he liked it, but he chose not to be a heroin addict because he had seen the destruction that it caused to people and their families.

So I asked him, did he smoke because there was some big hit to be had from smoking tobacco, and he replied that it was more of a relief than a hit. Then he admitted that there was no real describable hit, and he also acknowledged that he was always trying to cut back his tobacco consumption. Up to 80 per cent of smokers want to stop but they feel that they cannot, because there are certain cigarettes that they enjoy and they cannot do without them. Many smokers actually say that if they could choose to smoke only the cigarettes they really enjoyed, then they would be happy to carry on smoking. How many smokers can do that? As a smoker you cannot choose to smoke the ones you like because your addiction controls your choice. You may be able to hold out for some time, but if you consider yourself a smoker, at some point you will smoke and carry on smoking. Those cigarettes that you think you enjoy are the ones that you have made yourself wait for, so that the sense of relief is greater when you have them. The only real cigarette that you are ever truly going to enjoy is the last one you choose to smoke. You didn't wake up one day and choose to be a smoker, just as no one decides to become a heroin addict.

You become a smoker because you are targeted by tobacco dealers' clever cigarette design and marketing. When tobacco advertising was more relaxed in the western world, some cigarette posters were deliberately set at an appropriate height for young children. It's no surprise that 80 per cent of smokers start before the age of 18.

Once you have understood all the trappings of tobacco, you will be able to make the choice you want. Real choice comes when you have sufficient information and are free to make the decision. When you buy a pack of cigarettes, it doesn't come with a manual or an agreement that you have to sign. When you buy drugs from a pharmacy, the chemist and the doctor have studied for years to appreciate the purpose and effects of the drug they are dispensing before you put it in your mouth. You should get an encyclopaedia with every pack of cigarettes, or at least a book explaining what you are letting yourself in for. The way things are going, you may have to sign a lengthy agreement created by the tobacco lawyers before you become a smoker, just to make sure that you will not sue them. Who is going to explain that agreement to the many smokers under 12?

Solution 6

The only real enjoyment that you will ever get from smoking is when you stop.

7

The highs and lows of smoking

No one starts off their smoking life on 20 cigarettes a day, or as a chain smoker on four packs a day. We all start off on a daily few and then build up either to the amount we allow ourselves to smoke or to the amount we have time to fit in. Many smokers never really allow themselves to smoke as much as their bodies crave. Only very strong smokers can handle smoking more than 60 a day. I use the word 'strong' because to smoke 60 or more a day, you have to have well-built lungs just to keep going with that lack of oxygen in your body and all that poison building up in your system.

The only time that the average smoker (who smokes 10–20 cigarettes a day) gets to appreciate what it is like to let go completely of their smoking inhibitions is when they go out and have a few drinks. Most of us who drink alcohol have found it easy to get through a pack of cigarettes before the end of the evening, especially on a big night out. But, as I said, no one starts off as a heavy or even moderate smoker; they have to build up to it.

Until very recently, part of the advertising on a pack of smokes used to include whether it was a high- or low-tar cigarette. This information was banned because it was seen as misleading, making customers believe they were smoking a less harmful cigarette if they smoked a brand described as low tar. When I felt guilty about not giving up smoking, I used to try to smoke Silk Cut cigarettes instead of my normal Marlboro. When Marlboro Lights came out, I felt that they were the perfect brand to smoke as they were somewhere between the two; and when Camel Lights came on the market I felt even more accommodated in my choice of smokes. Well done, you guys and girls at the marketing departments of the tobacco companies!

Nowadays, cigarettes come with their tar content shown by a scale of strength in milligrams. This is measured by an automated machine that draws air through the cigarette at a set amount. Unfortunately, this machine does not resemble the design of your brain, lungs and lips. Moreover, the machine does not have an addiction to nicotine and suffer insecure cravings as you regularly do.

When you suck on a cigarette you get out as much as you need to quell the desire in your nicotine brain. Whether you suck harder, smoke more, cover the filter holes, smoke until you reach the butt of the filter, have a fatter cigar or pipe, or just take longer drags, your body tells you when you are topped up. Once that is sorted, you can carry on for a bit until you get interrupted again and need to have a quick fix.

Most smokers wait for some time or delay getting that fix, perhaps because they do not have the chance to pop out for a smoke. This means that at some point in every day smokers experience the cravings of withdrawal that make them reach for another smoke. The last time you were in a situation where you could not smoke, I bet you dealt with it sensibly and waited until you could.

So whatever brand you smoke or whatever type of tobacco you buy, whether with or without filters, you are still getting screwed like all the other smokers. Just because you smoke ultra lights, don't think that you are doing yourself any favours; you will suck out the amount of smoke, tar and nicotine that your body wants.

As your drug of choice happens to be addictive, it means that over time your body will build up a tolerance to its intensity. So to satisfy those little cravings or to control them, you will either have to smoke more or to go through ever-increasing nicotine cravings. Two types of people never have to experience these annoying withdrawal sensations. The first are very heavy smokers who never get on a bus, plane or train, go to the cinema or a restaurant or ride a motorbike. The other type who do not have to put up with this self-inflicted misery are people who do not smoke. Luckily it is very easy to deal with the physical cravings, as you have done almost every day of your life. Dealing with the mental cravings requires a little bit of effort on your part, but still a lot less effort than you have put into turning yourself into a smoker.

Addiction

We all know that smoking is addictive but most smokers feel that addiction is just one element of the cigarette experience and not the whole reason that they smoke. We use the word 'addict' to describe people who crave too much chocolate, but we also use it to describe the full-time burglar who is only stealing to pay for his addiction to crack. If you were to put your addiction to smoking somewhere on a scale between the extremes of the chocoholic and the drug addict, where would you come? If this is your very first attempt at stopping smoking, you might put yourself at the lower end of the addiction scale, whereas the majority of those who have tried to give up many times with no conclusive result would place themselves up there with the hard-core drugs user.

In my earlier fruitless attempts to quit smoking I could sometimes be found going through a teabag-stained bin at home, looking for soggy cigarette butts that I could dry out and get a couple of drags out of. Because I knew what I was like when I was trying to quit, when I threw away tobacco or cigarettes at home I would flush them down the toilet just to make sure I would not be tempted to try to roll a smoke out of binned tobacco. Hopefully you have not sunk that low, but even if you have, it's not something that you will have to put up with in the future.

Your relationship with nicotine and all the other harmful chemicals present in your cigarette resemble an intolerable marriage that will only be resolved when you split up. In your unfulfilled marriage you are risking everything – your health, your sanity, your money and your overall well-being – all for a big slap in the face. Addiction is when you believe that what you crave at that moment is absolutely necessary for you to exist and carry on.

Suppose I came up to you in the street today and offered you a year's free holiday anywhere in the world with all expenses paid and all you had to do was never smoke again. Could you do it? Could you confidently guarantee that you would never put another cigarette or cigar or any other form of nicotine in your system? Surely a year's free holiday is going to be more tempting than the joy you get from smoking? The day that you could give that guarantee is the day you are not an addict to the weed. The day you can say yes and accept such a prize is the day you are free to do what you want for the rest of your life.

I have been offered more than free holidays if I could promise to help someone to stop smoking. Unfortunately, the only person who can stop you smoking is you. Fortunately, what I *can* say is that you can easily stop smoking if you are willing to accept that you are not in control of your addiction and that you never will be as long as you continue to be an addict. What makes you an addict is the drug that you consume. What makes you free from all the uncomfortable feelings and situations is realizing that you never wanted to be a nicotine junkie in the first place. That way we can start to deal with all the misconceptions and dishonest answers you have been using to get along with your drug habit.

If you do not class yourself as an addict, why is it that at some points in your life you told yourself that you did not want to smoke but still carried on? If you are not an addict, why are all these millions of people able to carry on their happy lives without smoking and you are not? Do you think they are wandering around thinking, 'I wish I could take up smoking'?

If, today, I could inject you with a drug that cost only one thousand pounds and would stop you ever having another cigarette, would you pay the money or not? When I was a smoker, even though I could not have afforded it I would have paid ten times that amount if I could have been certain that such a drug would work. Luckily, this book is not that expensive. If you read it carefully and have an open mind about your relationship with smoking, you should have no problem beating your addiction once and for all.

It is never too late or too early

However young or old you are or feel, you know that your life would be better if you did not smoke. That is why you are reading this book. Many young people tell themselves they will give up when they are 30 or when they get their own place. Many people in their more mature years tell me they will quit the day they die. They have tried to stop and failed many times. They console themselves with the belief that they were obviously 'born to be a smoker'. No one was ever born to be a smoker; remember that, except for in a few parts of the world, smoking tobacco has only been around for the past 500 years.

Many people return to the excuse 'I am a smoker and I like it', or something similar, because they are unable to find anything better. Do you think some people are just more prone to smoking and some are not? Is it part of your chemical make-up? At certain times in history, more than half the population in some countries have smoked. In parts of the western world, smoking has greatly declined because people are better informed and have more knowledge about what they do. If I had written this book 100 years ago I might have been sued by the tobacco companies, and the government would probably have supported the companies.

Thankfully, in many western countries smoking is on the decline because the truth about all the harmful effects of smoking is common knowledge. That's great if you are thinking about whether you should take up smoking, but not too helpful if you have been doing it for the past 40 years. Can you teach an old dog new tricks? Of course you can, as long as you are prepared to question yourself and accept the truth about yourself.

I once helped a young female colleague, aged 19, to stop smoking. Some time ago she mentioned that she had visited her doctor because of her asthma. The doctor told Liz that there were some people who could get away with smoking and some that could not. She was one of the types that could not get away with it. The sooner she stopped, the sooner her breathing was going to improve. With encouragement from me and others, she stopped and is feeling very much better. Another example is a guy at the gym called Terry. He is in his early fifties, physically very robust and a definite character at any social event. He has 'got away' with smoking for over 40 years. Now he mainly smokes cigars and makes an effort to confine his smoking to the evenings. He is quite an active person and knows that if he smokes too much his physical capacities are impaired. If you ask him why he still carries on, he says in a jovial rough voice that, 'I have got this far and I do not smoke half as much as I used to'. If I ask him whether he would stop if I could make him do so just by clicking my fingers, he replies, 'Of course I would but it is not as easy as that'.

Whether you are young or old, have been smoking for six months or 60 years, it is easy to stop if you start off on the right foot and with the right key. As a smoker, there is a part of your brain that has not been used for some time. Think of it as a room with a closed door. Behind that door is the way you used to feel before you started smoking. This state of mind existed for all of us; it has just been a while since we opened that door. Many of us find it hard to remember that far back, but we know that a time existed when smoking had no control or effect on our lives. Even though most of us were young at that time, we were happy and content and never felt the need to set fire to our lungs. You are going to open that door and switch the light on in that room and when you do, you will never have to close it again. Once the light is on in that room, the part of the brain that makes you think you want to smoke disappears. As long as you keep that door open, the desire will never return.

Once you have thought about stopping smoking there is no real excuse not to go ahead with it. It would be stupid not to. There are many reasons to stop that you can use as inspiration and encouragement and we shall look at these throughout this book. The most obvious point by far is: if you do not want to smoke, why should you have to? The answer to that, whatever age you are or however long you have been smoking, is that you do not. You do not have to smoke.

Solution 7

Before you started smoking you were content and never suffered cravings or a sense of emptiness. Once you clear the nicotine out of your system, that feeling of contentment returns.

8

But I really enjoy smoking

We have already seen that smoking is a drug addiction. That is the main reason why it is so difficult to quit. Another part of the problem with stopping is that we often associate a cigarette with some of the most pleasurable times in our lives: spending time with friends; sitting over a coffee watching the world go by; taking a break at work; reaching for a glass of wine after eating a delicious meal. But remember that those times are enjoyable because of what you are doing and who you are with, not because you are sucking poisonous smoke into your lungs.

Cigarettes, pipes and rolling or chewing tobacco are just the tools that tobacco manufacturers use to get nicotine into your system. Everything from the advertising to the marketing, the sleek and slender design of the cigarette, the trendy and colourful design of the packaging, even the length of a cigarette and the number put into a pack, have been designed to keep you smoking. Tobacco companies are like any other business; their aim is to make money. The problem is that they are peddling an addictive drug that is 100 per cent guaranteed to age you more quickly, damage your health, reduce your lifespan and take away some of your quality of life – and, in addition, make you stink. But that's all right because you think that you really enjoy it, and you enjoy it so much that the pleasure of smoking far outweighs the fact that you are detracting from the quality of your life just to keep tobacco companies making billions. Because that is the only real benefit of smoking!

Another way of getting nicotine into your bloodstream is to chew nicotine gum. Over the years the flavour of this gum has improved, but no one would choose to buy it in preference to regular gum for its taste or its price. Many hardened smokers will say that they tried the gum to help them stop smoking, but having tasted it they took up smoking again just to give up the gum. It is obvious that when you have gum or nicotine patches you don't feel the need to smoke. Most people (and I include myself) who have tried to smoke while wearing an extra-strong nicotine patch feel as if they are being poisoned well before they get to the end or even halfway through a cigarette.

If it were legal, do you think that cigarette companies would make sweets with nicotine in them? Of course they would! And remember that nicotine is a poison; it has no benefit to the human body other than making you want more of it because it is addictive. Young people are still targeted by tobacco companies; if they get hooked early, there is more chance of them smoking for longer. There are tighter controls on tobacco advertising than ever before, but obviously we as smokers are the worst kind of advert because we make it seem acceptable. Many smokers inform me of the great virtues of smoking and scoff at the exaggerated claims they believe the medical world makes about their favourite hobby. They delight in telling me that if they could not smoke their favourite brand, they would not smoke at all. Rubbish! Any smoker who has tried to quit or go for a long time without smoking knows that once you decide to postpone giving up (again . . .) you will smoke anything, including tea bags, freshly cut grass and even elephant droppings, as long as it has some nicotine in it.

Let me put this across in a more unsavoury way. Imagine the most disgusting tasting substance you could put in your mouth and chew. People who know me would tell you that for me it's a fine line between trifle and my own excrement (especially if I have just been force-fed trifle). I am even gagging at writing the word 'trifle'! However, so we can all be on the same wavelength I am going to use trifle as my example and I apologize if you find this offensive but there is a strong point I want to put across.

Imagine you were stuck on a desert island where all you could eat was the most horrible dessert of trifle, but unknown to you it had been contaminated with the poison nicotine. Every day you decide to go without food, but every day your innate instinct for survival means you end up eating the trifle. Even though it makes you choke and gag at every mouthful, you force it down because you have no choice and you vow that if you ever get off this island you will never eat this particular foodstuff again.

After two months of living on dessert, a fishing boat passes by and you are saved! With a smile on your face, you stick your fingers up at the island and throw your dessert spoon overboard.

Once on board you have a chat with the chef and he prepares a top fish dinner with all your favourite vegetables. Your stomach has never been so happy but once your food has gone down, you still do not feel satisfied. You have this strange craving for a combination of cream, custard, mixed fruit, jelly with hundreds and thousands sprinkled on top. You can't believe what your brain is telling you: you want trifle! The worst substance known to your body and your brain tells you that you have a craving for it. You go to bed with this slightly annoying, irritable, nagging feeling, but you cannot quite put your finger on it.

You wake up in the morning with this slight craving and when you get to the galley on the boat you beg the chef to make you trifle. You sit staring at the trifle in front of you, spoon at the ready. The one substance you never wanted to put in your body ever again and you have just ordered an extra helping; but your brain is saying, 'Just one mouthful, go on, you know you want to'. Finally you dive in and finish the bowl in seconds, nearly choking on every spoonful. As soon as you have finished, you eat another bowl, and then another, until your stomach is ready to burst, but you are still not getting the satisfaction you need. What you don't realize is that because there is no nicotine in the trifle, your pangs of addiction are never quite satisfied. Fortunately, it doesn't take long for the nicotine to leave your bloodstream and soon your mental craving for nicotine (and trifle) subsides and disappears.

As adults, at least we have an understanding of addiction even though some of us have not experienced it. Unfortunately, it is harder for young people to understand. In their minds, if their body has a craving for something and they can get hold of it, they will have it. Look at kids with sugary sweets. As adults we know that too much sugar or fats are bad for us, but as kids or teenagers we don't care. We want the calorific fix of fats and the sweet fix of sugar, even though most of the calories lack any nutritional or health benefit.

Some smokers may have tried to cut out smoking by switching to herbal cigarettes. If you have not experienced this delight, then find yourself a pile of old rubber tyres and some petrol, sprinkle some jasmine and stale potpourri over the pile and

NICOTINE,
NOT TO BE
TRIFLED WITH!

set light to it. Get your head right over the fire and take a few deep breaths – only then will you come close to the experience of herbal cigarette smoking. To approximate those pompous smokers who will only smoke their favoured brand, you can sprinkle on your favourite brand of tea instead of the potpourri. I, along with others, have tried the herbal cigarette route, but I have yet to meet anyone who has managed to finish a whole pack. Please don't contact me if you have; you need more help than this book delivers.

You could put the sweetest flavours in your herbal cigarette, but without the nicotine you would not quell the desire for more nicotine, and as we know nicotine has no benefits. Luckily, it does not take long for nicotine to leave our system or for the very mild physical withdrawal symptoms to subside. Moreover, in the initial stages of stopping smoking it is more important that we prompt our minds with all the positive effects of being free from smoking and remind our habitual subconscious not to pick up that cigarette. It is your mind that is going to stop you smoking, because once it fully realizes how damaging smoking is to every aspect of your life, it becomes easy to never want to smoke again.

Throughout this book you will find many positive reasons why you will not want to or feel the need to smoke ever again. I have my own mental prompts that helped me to realize that I hate smoking and would never want to take it up again, even if you paid me. I am not saying my prompts will be your prompts, but you will find suggestions and phrases to help you create your own, and some blank pages at the end of the book where you can write them down. Please use these prompts to remind yourself that smoking is not for you and never will be again.

 Solution 8

If the tobacco companies force-fed you camel droppings with nicotine in them, you would end up thinking you liked them.

9

How much do you enjoy smoking?

All you need for the following little self-test is to realize that the reason you smoke is because of nicotine, and to use your imagination. If you have not reached the conclusion that you smoke because of the withdrawal symptoms and craving for nicotine, or that you still smoke because you enjoy the action of smoking, then you must:

1 read previous chapters in the book

2 purchase a pack of herbal cigarettes and smoke said pack

3 if herbal cigarettes are not available, find some tea bags, empty the contents into one large Rizla paper and light it up

4 try all three of the above.

Now imagine that you were no longer allowed to smoke because it had been made illegal and it was impossible to get hold of tobacco. If this is difficult, spare a thought for the smokers who lived in the 17th century. In 1617 in Mongolia the use of tobacco was punished with the death penalty, so people were literally dying for a smoke. In 1633, Sultan Murad IV of Turkey ordered as many as 18 executions a day of people who had been caught smoking. In late 17th-century Russia you could get off lightly with a flogging, have your lip slit so you could not suck, be sent to Siberia or be sentenced to death. Even in colonial America, where tobacco later became the most lucrative crop, the governments in some colonies would only allow smoking once a day, and never in public or even in the presence of others. What an effort just to have one smoke, although there was no stipulation on how long the smoke could last. Some people probably had very big pipes!

It may be slightly easier to imagine that you could not get hold of tobacco but you could still get your nicotine fix through other devices:

a a syringe with a big thick needle

b an intravenous drip

c a suppository

d nicotine-flavoured chocolate.

Put these four devices in order of preference, with the favourite first and the least favoured last. I am hoping that your first choice would be chocolate. For me the order would be:

1 nicotine-flavoured chocolate

2 a syringe with a big thick needle

3 an intravenous drip

4 a suppository.

So if nicotine-flavoured chocolate existed but smoking was banned, there is a good chance that you would still be a nicotine addict – and perhaps a little fatter from your 20-a-day habit. If the chocolate option is taken away, the chances are that most of us would stop being a nicotine addict straight away. The amount of hassle and discomfort would be enough for us to say, 'Why bother?'. Can you really imagine shooting up at the dinner table after eating at your favourite restaurant? And choice 'c' would probably put everyone off their desserts!

By now you are probably saying all of this does not matter because I can smoke and it is not illegal to do so. But wait. You agreed at the beginning of this chapter that smoking was only the device by which you received your drug, and without the nicotine in the cigarette you would not smoke. So you do not want to be a nicotine addict, and smoking has no point without the nicotine in it. Why do you still want to smoke?

The problem is that you still may not have married the two concepts – of nicotine addiction and smoking – together. You have been smoking for so long that you associate smoking with everything you do, especially the pleasant situations when you can sit back, have a drink, relax in a comfy chair, have a chat with a friend on the phone, have that first warm drink of the day or that first ice-cold one in the evening. Of course you do; those times when you sit back and relax are your perfect time to savour and enjoy relieving the pain of needing a smoke. When you see non-smokers sitting back and relaxing, do they look like they are missing out on something by not breathing in smoke? Of course not.

Essentially, the reason why we make ourselves smoke is a poisonous drug called nicotine. But when you hide the drug in a cloud of smoke, you associate the physical act of smoking with a pleasurable experience. Part of that is not only down to the relief you feel from alleviating withdrawal symptoms by having a smoke, but also to the perception of smoking as an enjoyable, glamorous, social, mature, cool, sophisticated act.

I would like you to think of some positive images that you associate with smoking from any age in your life. These can be situations or people that are close to you, or they may be old adverts or perhaps famous people you have seen smoking. Write these down if it helps. Also make a note of why these seemed like positive situations at the time.

Here are some of mine.

▶ When I was younger, hanging out with older boys and the adventure of trying something that I knew I should not do.

▶ Watching the movie stars of my youth, such as John Wayne, Clint Eastwood, Sylvester Stallone, Robert de Niro, Al Pacino and – OK, I hate to admit it – John Travolta, do their thing while having a smoke.

- The famous image of Audrey Hepburn smoking her cigarette in a holder while looking stunning, beautiful and elegant in the film *Breakfast at Tiffany's*.

- The Marlboro man. For those unfamiliar with the advertising campaign, this was a rugged, good-looking American who smoked Marlboro cigarettes. He was attractive, and looked tough but cool while hanging out in the wild west.

- No one over the age of 30 could forget the adverts showing how fantastic it was to smoke a Hamlet cigar as you were about to face your impending doom.

- The first ice-cold beer at the beginning of a two-week holiday.

- Two hours of great sex with the second ice-cold beer at the beginning of a two-week holiday and, oh I nearly forgot, the cigarette.

This list could go on and continue to reinforce the fact that even though we have decided that we want to stop smoking, we still find it hard just to stop and move on with our lives. We still associate smoking with positive memories. We believe that we would miss out on a lot of the pleasures in life if we did not smoke. This could not be further from the truth.

Your brain is the cleverest piece of equipment on this planet. It regulates millions of different actions within a split second, without you having to think about it. When we are thirsty, it lets us know we need more fluids; if we are dehydrated, it stops excreting fluids to conserve liquid. If we are too hot, it regulates our temperature by sweating or letting us know we need a drink. When we are tired, it tells us to eat particular food groups to replenish energy, or to rest and build up our strength. When we are running low on nicotine, it gives us a little reminder to have a smoke.

With one exception, if we were to leave any of these functions unattended for too long, we would end up in very dire and uncomfortable states. Too much heat in our bodies and we would collapse. Not enough food in our system and we would not move. Without rest we would eventually just keel over. No nicotine in our systems and what? Perhaps you might be a little bit grumpy and experience a slight empty feeling for a while. But nowhere near as uncomfortable as when you are bursting to go to the toilet; not as unpleasant as when you are feeling hungry or thirsty. In fact, most smokers I speak to will go without a cigarette if they are feeling thirsty until they get a drink, so as not to have that dry throat sensation. When you do stop smoking, for a while there is that empty feeling as if you were a little bit hungry, but there is no chance of you passing out.

Your brain has spent many years having its little fix – anywhere from five to 100 times a day – and every time it gets its fix, it tells you everything is fine for a little while. When you go without your fix, it keeps nagging until finally the desire disappears or you have your fix. Once you have got rid of the craving, the reason you go back to smoking three weeks down the line is that your memory still associates the smell of a freshly lit cigarette with all those false pleasurable associations that you wrote down earlier. Not, though, if you remember to tell your memory – that is your brain – that you never wanted to smoke. You need to un-condition all of those unreal situations and excuses about why you ever smoked and see them for what they are. You are lying to yourself that you're not a nicotine junkie. Indeed, you are not even getting a hit or a buzz out of smoking – just relieving the pain from withdrawal. You get a bigger hit out of taking in a few big breaths of oxygen than you do from a cigarette.

Let's have a quick recap, just to make sure that you never wanted to smoke, and answer these questions:

1 Would you recommend smoking to anyone in your family?

2 Do you hope that your children take up smoking?

3 Do you think that you would smoke if there were no nicotine in tobacco?

4 Do you believe that people who smoke look sophisticated or cool when they smoke?

5 If I offered you £10,000 in cash or an alternative of £20,000-worth of cigarettes, would you take the payment in cigarettes?

6 Do you believe that smoking is good for your health?

7 Would you like me to take up to 15 years off your life?

8 Would you like me to burn at least five pounds of your money every day?

9 Do you really like being a drug addict?

10 Do you like not being in control of a part of your life?

11 Do you think that tobacco companies care whether you live or die?

12 Is there a real benefit to you smoking?

13 Do you like the idea of tobacco companies having control over how you spend a portion of your life?

14 Are you fed up with making excuses about why you still smoke?

15 If you could click your fingers this minute and never want to have a cigarette again, would you click your fingers?

16 Do you think that your life would be better for not smoking?

17 Can you think of anything to do with the extra energy, money, time and positive attitude that come with not being a smoker?

18 Do you think that cutting down just prolongs the whole painful event of smoking?

19 Does the sensation of feeling free and more in control of your life sound at all appealing?

20 Are you responsible for the actions you take in your life?

Key point

You lose the empty feeling of needing a cigarette when you stop putting nicotine in your system. You lose the desire to smoke when you realize that smoking creates that empty feeling.

Nicotine replacement therapy

Do you know what I worry about sometimes? That on my gravestone they will write in big black letters: 'Too Little Too Late'. You know the feeling: I should have spent more time with my family; I should have been a better father; I could have been better at my job; I could have been fitter; I could have been more creative and made more effort; so often I took the easy route; my life should have been more fulfilling. So this is the big question. **The next step I take – does it lead me to where I want to go or leave me further away?**

Many times when I could have chosen a more important path I opted for a quick-fix stimulant to get my satisfaction, and it got me through. That might have been something as mundane as putting the kettle or TV on, instead of practising the piano or ringing the bank to sort out a problem. Have you done the same? Perhaps you have avoided making a phone call to mend a fragile relationship or sending off your CV to further your career. Instead we pour ourselves a drink, sit back and tell ourselves we'll do it when we are feeling better. That quick fix seems to make it easier but tends to leave us with a stronger sense of guilt. I will just have a smoke and then I will see how I feel. That placebo, whether it is smoking, booze, shopping, overeating, sex, drugs or whatever, numbs us enough to avoid immediately taking the required step.

If the feeling was a craving for warmth, food, water, sleep, protection or relief from fear that would make sense. But if it's somewhere between boredom and absolute despair, do we often neither understand nor deal with it? You know the situation. I just don't want to deal with it right now, so I will find some form of self-medication that gets me through, even though I know deep down it will leave me feeling more empty than before. And what do we do when we feel even emptier? Go straight back to our 'medicine' but in search of a stronger hit.

Have our lives become corrupted with too much choice, or have our brains been commercialized to the point where we can never have enough? Do we expect or want too much or can we not see the wood for the trees? What seemed to satisfy us last week is not enough this week. How often do we stop and appreciate what we have and what is around us?

I know this may sound a bit 'mid-life crisis' but I often envy farmers. I am not likely to become a hard-working farmer and I appreciate the various problems they face, but I imagine their lives have a rhythm with nature, a structure and a sense of purpose. They have to follow a pattern of life that is intertwined with the seasons and the weather, along with life and death. They have to think, but essentially they have to do. They won't let their crops or livestock down just because they are not in the mood. They would not neglect to get up early to milk the cows because they stayed up late playing PlayStation. If it's raining and sheep are lambing in the fields, they cannot just put the kettle on and open a packet of doughnuts. They have, and I imagine they want, to go and help whatever they have created to grow and move forward to the next stage of life. I suppose what I envy is the sense of unquestioning purpose and structure that underpins their lives. Now I may be looking through rose-tinted glasses, but when I spent holidays on my aunt and uncle's farm, I used to love getting up early and helping my uncle milk the cows or sticking on my boots and fixing the fences in a storm. It never felt like a chore; it never felt like work; you just had to get on with it. I am sure my cousins, who did it day in and day out, might not agree with me. I suppose the point I am trying to make is: 'Less thinking, more action'. Structure is a good thing; it stops us wandering when we become lost in our feelings. I hope you would agree that we feel much better when we get on and do something rather than sitting there thinking about it. If you think about something for too long, you can either talk yourself out of it or scare yourself into doing something a lot more pointless. As human beings, we need to feel we are moving forward and creating a better future for ourselves and those for whom we care. Whatever stage of life you are at, stopping smoking is going to give you more energy and a greater sense of well-being. I'm counting on your wanting to add to your life, so here is the next key point to add to your armoury.

Key point

Does your next action hurt you or help you?

Now this may seem too big a mountain to climb or you may not even know where to start. So let's try this next exercise and see where it leaves us.

Life assessment

Draw a circle and then draw four lines through the middle, cutting the circle into eight even pieces of cake. On the edge of the circle, at the end of each line, put one of the following headings:

- Family
- Relationships
- Money
- Health

- Work
- Spirituality
- Home
- Friends

Taking the centre of the circle as zero, mark each line with 2, 4, 6, 8 and 10, with 10 being the outer edge of the circle. Add a mark on each line for how you would score that area of your life.

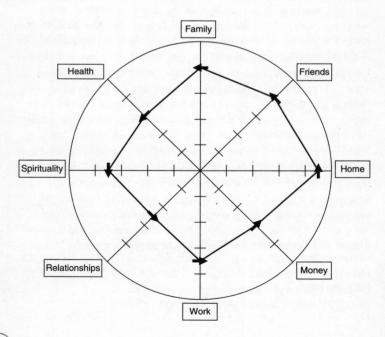

When you have done all eight, draw a line joining all the marks together. On the other side of the paper you have used for the diagram, write down your reasons for the scores you have given. Those words are whatever they mean to you and the scores are just how you are feeling today; but in case you are having trouble getting going, here is somebody else's results from the exercise.

I gave 'Family' a score of eight, as I feel I have all my family around me and we make the effort to do fun things when we get together. If I am in trouble or in need of help, I know they would always be there for me and they would never judge whatever I wanted to talk about.

'Relationships' scored five, because I have good honest relationships around me, but the way I have been feeling recently has made me selfish in the way I treat those relationships and I feel I am not making enough effort.

'Money' scored six as it is not a major worry. However, as a self-employed person with a daughter about to start school soon, I may need to increase my income, so money is in the back of my mind.

'Health' is OK and I try to exercise three times a week, but I could do with losing 10 pounds so I gave it a six.

'Work' is OK, and the challenge is to stay interested and encouraging in what I do and to look forward to see what I can add in the future, so I gave it a seven.

'Spirituality' I had to think about. I am not a religious person but I would say that I adhere to certain values such as Adventure, Creativity and Nurturing, and that when I am following them they enhance my life and those of others around me. I gave it a seven.

'Home' got a nine because I have all the people I need around me and I feel safe.

'Friends' got an eight, as I have good, longstanding friends that I can discuss anything with. It would be nice to have more of them living in the same country and not scattered around the world, but I make the effort to stay in touch and it is great when I do see them.

Once you have scored and written down your thoughts, decide which category, if you were to improve, would have the most positive effect on the others. It does not have to be the lowest scoring category.

The person above concluded that if they did more to improve their health, it would give them greater energy and a stronger frame of mind to make more effort in all the other areas. Even just going to bed earlier and laying off the alcohol a bit would mean that they could get out of bed in the morning with a positive outlook rather than needing a jump start from a bucket of coffee.

This simple exercise can be used often to assess what is going on in your life and highlight the areas where improvements will leave you feeling more satisfied.

Solution 9

Do the things that honestly leave you fulfilled. Realize that the important things in life are not things.

10

The benefits of smoking

In 2000, the world's largest tobacco company sent a detailed report to the government of the Czech Republic outlining the financial benefits to be derived from allowing heavy promotion of smoking in their country. It stated that the financial gain from tobacco taxes and premature deaths relating to smoking reduced the demands of older members of the community on social services. Basically, if these people are dead, you don't have to pay their pensions, housing benefit etc. The report was an in-depth study that covered many topics, but in a highly selective way that showed that the company's overriding purpose was financial gain. This chapter highlights some of the arguments in the report.

Increased costs

The report employed four main headings to cover the direct costs from diseases caused by smoking. These were:

- cardiovascular diseases

- respiratory diseases

- neoplasms (tumours)

- low birth weight and defects.

The report accepted that these diseases were up to four times more likely to occur in smokers and that such diseases were a direct result of smoking and secondary smoke. With these numbers it arrived at the increased cost of smoking to the government and Czech health service. The report also recognized that, on average, smokers took an extra week a year off work compared to non-smokers as a result of ill-health and hospital appointments. It did not, however, accept that smokers were less efficient at work due to cigarette breaks and lack of focus.

Increased savings

By identifying the number of smokers who went to an early grave the report calculated the amount of money saved by the government on pensions, health care and other social benefits as a result of these premature deaths. Losses in tax revenue from dead smokers were offset by arguments about reductions in unemployment and unemployment benefit.

Increased revenue

The report drew attention to the several duties and taxes paid by the tobacco companies and tobacco-related businesses. The high levels of profitability of tobacco companies compared to other firms meant that corporate taxation alone would generate an additional CZK 747 million a year for the government.

The sales pitch

The basic sales pitch contained in the report was: Figures for 1999 show that 22,000 deaths in that year were attributed to smoking. The subtext was: 'if you give us greater freedom to advertise and distribute our products, we could kill a lot more people than that'.

Profit and loss

Just for fun (or rather for impact) I would like you to imagine that you are one of the employees who has worked hard and enthusiastically to come up with this report. You come home to your four-year-old son and newly born baby daughter, who is being looked after by your lovely wife and your mother, who is staying for a month to help out. After finishing your tasty meal, all of you sit back at the dinner table to relax. You get out a big, fat cigar and light up. Grandma pulls out her ready rub and starts to pack it into her pipe. Your wife has already starting rolling herself a fat one and Junior is given some vanilla chewing tobacco which was free from work. The baby just lies there sucking in big gulps of secondary smoke. Ahhhhhhh, how relaxing!

'So what did you do at work today, love?' asks your wife.

'Just boring stuff. We put together some marketing files that will help us sell some more of our wonderful product,' you reply.

'Did it go well, dear?' asks your mother.

'I think so, I worked on trying to find a way of hiding the real figures for stillbirths and breathing difficulties in babies.'

'You are clever, Daddy,' says Junior.

'Well, son, if the truth be told I was a little disappointed with the fact that I could only prove that 22,000 people died from smoking in the Czech Republic in one year.'

'Don't worry, darling, I am sure you will think of something,' says your loyal wife.

'It is funny you said that, my beautiful wife, because on the way home I did a bit of brainstorming with Geoff from accounting.'

'What wonderful idea did you come up with this time, dear?' asks your mother.

'I thought I could interest the government in giving a tax incentive to young couples to persuade their ageing parents into doubling their cigarette consumption after retiring.'

'Ooh, you are a clever daddy,' squeals Junior.

'Shall I refill your pipe, Mother?'

This may come across like a sketch from *The Simpsons*, but it defies belief that people could put their products into such a sales package and still sleep at night. At least an arms dealer knows that clients are aware of what they are buying and what the weapons can do. The heroin dealer preparing £10 crack bags to sell to kids at least knows it's wrong and recognizes that there is a price to be paid if he gets caught.

Many of the figures and arguments in the report take no account of current and future developments in medical treatment. Nor are other factors considered. For example, in many countries in the developed world, older members of the population are becoming increasingly self-sufficient and relying less on state pension provision. Statistics in the report are selectively quoted to the advantage of the tobacco companies. Clearly, if people were spending less money on tobacco, they might be spending more on products that were less detrimental to themselves and to the Czech economy. These commodities

CLEVER DADDY

could also generate tax revenue. A healthy and reasonably affluent group of senior citizens can make a considerable contribution to the economy as well as providing a wealth of experience and input, for example, in terms of family support and charitable endeavour. No one should be encouraged to reduce, demean and diminish their lives simply to fund the profits of the tobacco companies.

Nothing in this report, or in the marketing of other tobacco companies, confronts the issue of the emotional and other cost to people who have to watch their loved ones suffer and die an early and unpleasant death.

The report data cited in this chapter are easily accessed at www.tobacco.org via a search for 'Public Finance Balance of Smoking in the Czech Republic'.

In 2004 the European Commission's Directorate-General for Health and Consumer Protection reported that one in seven deaths in Europe was smoking related. The Czech Republic already exhibits a higher than average rate of smoking deaths. The percentage of Czech men between the ages of 35 and 54 dying of lung cancer is higher than the European average. The rate of lung cancer in Czech women is also much higher than the European average. In many of the less developed and rapidly developing countries around the world the percentage of smokers is already very high. For example, China has over 300 million smokers. That's a lot of cigarettes. As more restrictions are imposed in the developed countries, international tobacco companies are targeting these still expanding markets.

Solution 10

Hands up those of you who in any way trust the companies that have been supplying you with your tobacco.

11

Why use willpower?

Many people who have given up smoking go on about how they still miss it. I have had people explain to me that they have not smoked a cigarette for ten years but they still like the distant smell of a freshly lit cigarette, wafting towards them when sitting outside a bar or restaurant, even when eating. My response to that is: 'Why don't you sit right next to the smoker while you are eating?' The answer is normally a look of disgust followed by 'Why would I want to put myself off my food?'.

How many people do you know who actually like to smoke while they are eating? Even most heavy smokers will stop smoking to eat. The smoker who has given up for many years yet craves the smell of smoke still has the brain of a smoker and their chances of returning to smoking are quite high. The type of people who make themselves stop smoking even though they think they like it are normally very strong-willed and disciplined people. I do not count myself as one of these, yet I miss smoking like I miss an extra-big hole in the head.

If you go down the willpower method of stopping smoking, you are always going to torture yourself a little, living in hope that one day you will go off smoking completely. Every time you see a smoker or get a faint whiff of a freshly lit cigarette, your brain is going to have to deal with the salivating desire to start smoking again. That is because you have not bothered to tell your brain the truth about smoking and you still think you miss it. If you are relying simply on self-discipline to get you through the rest of your life, it is going to be a painful experience. Remember to see smoking for what it is, an uncomfortable craving that your body does not like and does not need, and which makes you feel insecure and on edge.

Our sense of smell has a strong connection with our subconscious memory. Even if you have your eyes closed, you can tell what season it is. If it is about to rain, you can smell it in the air before it happens. An aroma you might not have smelled for years can be enough to trigger a memory from long ago. Tobacco companies know this, and part of the design and make-up of a cigarette is to make it smell and taste as pleasurable as possible to hide all the horrible stuff that is in it. When most of us think of an open fire, it gives us a sense of pleasure. We think of being warm and watching the flames dance in the fireplace, and the crackling sound as the sparks fly up the chimney. Maybe the thought even conjures up images of a thick rug and putting your feet up to relax while looking at the cold, crisp night through the window. The smell of an open fire is very pleasurable, and when you first smell an open fire it triggers off the idea in your brain that it is nice to be warm and comfortable. That mental memory is there to remind us how to stay warm and comfortable during times when it is cold or when the central heating has broken down.

Smoking is a 95 per cent mental addiction. What you think you are seeing or sensing when you come into contact with cigarette smoke is your subconscious brain telling it whatever you have programmed in. So if you have only been using willpower to stop yourself from smoking for many years, you have been telling yourself 'There is something that I want to do but I am not allowing myself to do it'. That must be the way horny monks spend the whole of their lives. Uncomfortable thought, don't you think?

To someone who is trying to use willpower alone to give up smoking, my question would be: 'Why do you have to make life so painful?'. It is no big secret to you that you do not want to smoke. The secret is that you never once enjoyed smoking; you just don't have that memory firmly sitting on top of and suffocating the old memory of 'I want a smoke'. The reason you are slow to accept this idea is that, as a person with strong willpower, you do not like to tell yourself that you have been getting it wrong for so many years. No one likes looking in the mirror and saying, 'Sucker'. Would it help you to get angry with yourself if someone from the tobacco company knocked at your door and screamed in your face 'GOT YOU'? If you think that one day you are going to wake up as a smoker and suddenly feel like not smoking again, you are wrong. If you are someone who is using willpower to stop smoking, you need to realize that all your pleasurable thoughts about smoking are false memories and excuses. Once you can do that, you can start to enjoy not having to smoke.

The biggest problem for people who are just using self-discipline to stop smoking is that they think of stopping smoking as a hard task to complete.

The people I know who use willpower to stop smoking are the most stubborn, hard-headed, strong, opinionated and thick-skinned people around. Now I am not saying those are bad qualities in a person. At the right time and in the right place these are useful and admirable traits. I would describe my wife as strong-minded, because she gets on with things when people around her are wasting their time gossiping and worrying about trivial things; most people who know my wife say about her, 'If you want something done, give it to Sue'. However, if you have not admitted the real reason for smoking yet and you are relying on your hard-headedness to see you through, you are just making life uncomfortable for yourself. If you want to torture yourself, buy a whip. If you want to stop wanting to smoke, then realize that you have been wrong about smoking for years.

If you know anyone who has stopped smoking through the willpower method, ask him or her if they think it is fantastic that they do not have to smoke any more and wait for their reply. If their reply starts with 'Yes but...', you know that they are still making their lives uncomfortable due to smoking. The whole reply will be something like 'Yes but I still miss smoking after dinner or over a coffee.'

Unfortunately, many people return to smoking if they are just using their self-control to keep their nicotine brain at bay. I know people who have not smoked for 11 years only to have smoked a cigarette one day and within a week be back on 20 a day. This often happens because of a traumatic experience, like the loss of a loved one or the end of a relationship. On the other hand, it can be that after 11 years of depriving yourself, you are thinking that all the smokers you see around you seem to be enjoying themselves, but not you. You say 'Stuff this' and grab the nearest cigarette and start puffing. If you are like me, you have done this before. For me, it was normally no longer than 11 days, or sometimes hours, before I got to that stage. Once you have taken a few drags on that first cigarette you start thinking, 'Why am I doing this?'. You have relieved any craving for nicotine in the first puff and now you are left with a sensation of 'Is that it?'. All this waiting and holding back, as you have built your smoking need into an event that should resemble a royal wedding, but it feels like you missed it.

A part of you thinks, 'Well, if this is what smoking does for me then it will be even easier for me to give up smoking next time'. That cigarette turns out to be a bit of a disappointment, because it did not deliver the big hit you were expecting. If you have not smoked for a long time, at most it will have made you feel a little light-headed and you might have noticed your heart rate increase slightly, but there were no gold dragons flying by or smoke-ring-blowing angels singing sweet music. Somehow, though, you still manage to finish the smoke and soon after you have another, just to confirm how horrible smoking is and that you will never want to do that again in the future. The nicotine is back in your system and very soon afterwards, unless you realize what is going on in your head, you are going to be feeling the irritations of needing your next fix and be wanting another smoke.

I know some people who have given up smoking solely using willpower. Their take on smoking is that they used to enjoy it, but they have decided they shall not and so they tell themselves not to do it even though they still miss it. These people tend to think everyone should be like them and that is the right way to go about it. They are normally very strong-willed people and you could describe them as stubborn. When you are a person who likes to believe that you are always in control of your life, it is hard to admit to yourself that you are, or have been, an out-of-control junkie who is partly controlled by a bit of weed. The problem is these people still miss smoking and every time they crave a smoke they go through the painful process of denial. So that is why I emphasize the point of seeing smoking for what it was or what it is. No one likes finding out they have been conned from an early age; no one likes finding out they were wrong about smoking, especially if you are the type of person who is always right.

If I went out to dinner at a restaurant and they served me a piece of uncooked, rancid meat, my brain would tell me exactly what it was – a stinking pile of flesh that I could do without putting into my digestive system. You could take that stinking mess, put it in a salad, mix it with grilled bacon to make it smell good and have it served in a fancy restaurant with mood music and dimmed lighting and you would still not hide the fact of what it is. Once you know what you are letting yourself in for by putting rancid meat in your system, however good it may taste, you know the end result. You would be sick and unwell for some time; the chances are that you would avoid that type of meat for a long time, if not forever, because your brain would be wary of suffering the same consequences.

However, if you do the same with addictive substances, even though you might be ill from taking too much, once the body starts to crave a particular substance, it seems to bypass all the common sense receptors in your brain.

If you walk down the street and see a half-filled syringe with heroin written on the side of it, would you rush to grab it and get your fix? Only if you are a heroin addict! The rest of us would see that needle for what it is, and we would try to kick it into the gutter to put it out of harm's way. Every non-smoker can see smoking for what it is, for how it affects you and what it does to your health and they never want to do it or start doing it again. In just the same way, almost all of us would never want to follow a piece of hot, melted crack cocaine around some warm tinfoil with a pipe. You are right to be scared of smoking. It is a pointless addiction, designed to trap you. But you need not be scared of taking up smoking again once you appreciate that you are not giving up anything.

The danger of relying on willpower to give up smoking is that you may still feel that smoking was a pleasurable experience. Once you know the true facts about smoking, you realize that this was never true.

Solution 11

Once your brain has answers to all the excuses, all you need to do is use it.

12

Your biggest weapon

Your brain

Your brain controls thousands of functions in your body each day. These range from the automatic functions of internal organs to the actions it takes in response to specific messages received from the various senses, such as touch and taste. This is clearly a highly multi-layered activity. When was the last time you had to think about breathing? How did your body know it was time to cough? How did you know it was time to have a drink? The brain keeps everything running through a highly complex system of chemical releases and electrical messages. In times of stress it tells us to rest; in times of illness it suggests means of repair so that we can keep functioning. As we grow up it stores information about the world we live in so that we can survive and be safe and yet also, if necessary, adapt to new circumstances. It helps us with simple tasks, such as crossing the road, and complex ones, such as learning to communicate in a different language.

Until recently the only way of looking at people's brains was to wait until they were dead and conduct an autopsy. Now scanning techniques such as fMRI (which measures brain activity by detecting associated changes in blood flow) and PET (which maps brain function by measuring the metabolism of glucose) can show us the brain at work. Some of the findings are remarkable. For example, we now know that between the ages of three and ten a child's brain is twice as active as an adult brain. It is also clear that the brain is essentially neuroplastic. Not only does it continue to establish and to lose neural pathways throughout life, it is also able to relocate functions. Thus, some patients who suffered an injury or stroke have been able to recover by relocating the function previously exercised by a damaged area to another part of the brain. The prefrontal cortex, the area at the front of the brain that distinguishes modern humans from their predecessors, is only fully developed and functional by our early twenties. This is what makes us mature adults. But smoking, like other drugs, increases the amount of dopamine in the brain. When this dopamine reaches the prefrontal cortex it can inhibit the activity of neurons there and render us immature once more. Do we want to be immature?

In the 21st century, rapid and unprecedented changes are taking place in the developed world. The causes are clear. Cellphones, emails, the internet, social networking sites and television ensure constant connectivity every hour of the day and night. Babies are born digital; teenagers have become screenagers. A 2009 study showed that more than 2,200 text messages are sent or received every month via a US teenager's phone. A 2010 Ofcom report showed that in the UK, 16 to 24-year-olds spend 6.5 hours a day on media and communication. We are becoming better at using the medium than processing its contents. We scan and skim, rather than concentrate and reflect. In consequence our brains are being rewired. Research shows that the higher-level brain functions of many young people are being damaged. Meaningful contact with other humans and with the natural world is diminished in the search for immediate, screen-based, sensory thrills. Our brains are becoming more wired to immediate satisfaction with a sense of 'I WANT IT NOW'.

Every life experience produces some type of memory in the brain. This may be very short-lived, but if you do something regularly the brain builds up more neural pathways and muscle memory so that it becomes second nature. Walking, throwing an object, riding a bike or driving a car are all actions that, once we can perform them, take no thought to do again. These actions and consequent reactions become ingrained in our memory. And when you are learning something, the learning process is always more effective if it is associated with pleasurable emotions. These emotions may be triggered by the interesting nature of the subject or by the input of a skilled and effective teacher.

Emotions are a very powerful learning tool, and if the emotion is very strong it can change our view of the way we see things. How many times have we said that we love doing something? But how many times have we really been in love? Most of us can remember those exact moments, as we have experienced a strong emotion created by a chemical reaction in our bodies that leaves an imprint in the brain.

So much for love; what about hate or fear? Take the case of someone who hates going to the dentist and has not been for the past five years, but has been suffering toothache for the past month. Most of us would have booked an appointment within the first week of the pain. But if you were frightened of going to the dentist, you would hold out and hope that the pain would go away. Most of us have suffered bad toothache at some time and we know how excruciating the pain can be, up to the point of not being able to sleep at night.

As this frightened person, you tell yourself it is not going to be that bad and after months of waiting you book in at the dentist the next day. On that day you're more than a little nervous. As you step into reception you can smell the clean, antiseptic, dentist smell. You sit in the waiting room with all these calm people reading their papers and wonder why they are not hyperventilating with the fear of being in the dentist's chair. You are amazed at the calmness of the six-year-old who has just stopped playing with his toy and is now walking towards consulting room number four. You even catch sight of the silver drill slung at the side of the seat as the young child sits in the chair, just before the dentist's assistant shuts the door. The sweat is now starting to build under your armpits and you glance around looking for similar tell-tale signs in other nervous victims. In your mind, they are hiding their fear better than you. You are now at the point of running away. You have told yourself that the pain in your mouth is going and you are starting to feel a lot better.

The lights flicker slightly as there is a drain in the power supply. Obviously they are having to use the extra big drill on the little boy – will he ever be the same again? That's it! You are off! You can tell the lady at reception that you forgot to lock your car and once out the door you are free to run for it. You are nearly at the door and luckily the receptionist has her back to you, filling the printer with paper. You take one last glance behind to make sure she is not after you. As you turn towards the door your heart almost skips a beat. That young boy is staring up at you; he has just stepped out of the consulting room and is smiling at you in a funny way. There is drool coming out of one side of his mouth and the other side of his mouth is half smiling. You can see his tongue poking from behind the big gap where his two front teeth were. What have they done to him?

Before you have time to scream, a firm arm is guiding you into consulting room number four and you are forced to sit in the big chair. The chair begins to recline; the door slams with a resounding locking sensation and the lights begin to flicker. Could this be the end?

Twenty minutes later you are right as rain. You thank the dentist for her gentle touch and efficiency and then you confidently stroll up to the receptionist to book for the hygienist and your next six-monthly appointment, casually mentioning that you will never leave it so long again to visit the dentist. That evening you are out with friends at a steakhouse chewing on some well-cooked piece of meat. You calmly remark to your friends that it had been a little while since you had been to the dentist and you were amazed at the advancements that had been made in dental care. You even make a joke that when you last went to the dentist they used a foot pump to power the drill and a boring story as an anaesthetic. What was all the fuss about?

We have all been in similar situations – whether it be at the dentist, waiting to take an exam or driving test, next in line for an interview or audition, or going over the notes for our first big public speech. We probably all have our own 'dentist story' of an occasion that seemed such a big deal beforehand and then afterwards we wondered why we got so uncomfortable and bothered. Once we have been through such an experience, we tell our brains to remind ourselves not to worry so much next time. We put that memory into the back of our minds until we need to use it again.

So, for example, the next visit to the dentist does not make us so nervous. We rationalize what will actually happen and are quite pleased that there are people out there willing to stick their latex-gloved hands in our orifices in the cause of our better health. Once we have told our brain that there is no big ordeal we know how to deal with the situation. Our brain tells us there is nothing to be afraid of; indeed, the sooner we see the dentist, the sooner everything will get better.

Your brain is the biggest weapon you can use in the battle against smoking. By now you should be coming round to the idea that there is an identifiable cause of your craving for a cigarette. That cause is nicotine. The way to remove the craving for cigarettes is to stop putting nicotine into your bloodstream. Most people find that once they stop smoking the craving for cigarettes disappears within a week or two. It may take longer for some, and there is no doubt that during the initial period of nicotine withdrawal the craving may increase. That is when you need to use your brain to tell yourself four truths:

▶ that initially the craving will be strong because you have become nicotine dependent

▶ that you may also need to break associated habits – for example, in the past when you got tense or anxious your first reaction was to reach for a cigarette

▶ that if you do give in at this point you will have to begin the whole nicotine withdrawal process again

▶ that you can stop smoking; millions of people have done so and they are all leading better and healthier lives as a result.

When I look at a cigarette I see it for what it is, something that would make me feel uncomfortable for a couple of weeks and stinks – a bit like a week's supply of trifle-flavoured laxatives; as you may remember, I have a hatred of trifle. On the other hand, I have a great fondness for chocolate oatmeal cookies, or as most of you know them, Hobnobs. When I look at an extra-large milk-chocolate packet, my mouth starts to salivate and I have visions of dipping each milky, chunky, sweet biscuit into my tea and then putting it all into my mouth in one go. But many years of this practice have taught me that eating the extra-large packet with one cup of tea may taste great but normally leaves me feeling slightly sick and uncomfortable; far more uncomfortable than the withdrawal symptoms of nicotine. (I now limit myself to the smaller packs and remind myself to try to share a bit more.) Now, I am not saying that chocolate Hobnobs are the same as smoking. I am saying that although I may still be initially attracted to a large packet of chocolate Hobnobs, my brain tells me that the result of eating them all would not produce the pleasant effect that I might hope for. Instead, it would make me feel unwell.

Toothache is probably 20 times more uncomfortable than the relatively slight craving for nicotine. Indeed, many people think it would be easier to stop smoking if the withdrawal symptoms were a lot more uncomfortable – stomach cramps, diarrhoea, vomiting, cold sweats and nightmares, for example. This may seem strange but some smokers believe that were such dramatic effects to occur, once these had passed they would know they had cracked it. That might help with the first of the four truths listed above, but not with the second – that of association. Smokers believe that their habit is a relaxing pleasure which it is worth taking some risks for, when in reality it has been an unhealthy annoyance for their own bodies and for the bodies of those around them. Non-smokers are the truly relaxed people.

It comes as no surprise to learn that 83 per cent of smokers start before they are 20 years of age. Tobacco companies know that the younger people are when they hook them, the longer they are likely to smoke. Young people are less informed and more image-conscious. They may think little about the future and do not worry whether they will still have the use of both lungs and both legs by the time they are 45. Understandably, their aim is to live life now and in the immediate future. So if the tobacco companies can catch you young enough, by the time you realize you do not want to smoke, part of your brain registers not smoking as missing out on a particular pleasure in life. Every time you feel a little uneasy you reach for a smoke and that relieves the uneasy withdrawal symptoms. But if you had known then what you know now, you would never have smoked cigarettes in the first place.

Subconscious fear

Fear is a very powerful and useful emotion that plays a leading part in keeping us alive. Our memories of fear are the reason we have survived as a species; if our ancestors had not run away from animals that could have killed them, we would not be here today. As children we learn that hot things burn. Adults tell us so, we see examples – a bonfire in the garden, water boiling in a saucepan on the cooker – and perhaps, if we are unlucky, we actually get burned by picking up something hot or by staying too long in the sun. Accidents like this or other stressful happenings can produce phobias that remain with us until we understand and confront them.

I have a friend who is very clever, intelligent and rational, but is scared to death of baked beans. When baked beans are placed in his vicinity he will start to shake and sweat, and if you actually put the baked beans in front of him he would run out the door. I discovered this once when we were at a local café and someone accidentally served beans with his bacon and egg. I had to send the food away before he would come back and sit down. The reason for this phobia is that as a young child he was violently sick after eating baked beans and it has haunted him ever since. (I must admit that I feel the same way about Special Brew beer and Malibu, especially if you mix them together.)

Interestingly, he will eat dried beans with tomato sauce on the same plate, as he knows that he would not have a reaction to them. Yet so strong is his fear of feeling so sick again that he will not go anywhere near baked beans. Obviously, being sick is an uncomfortable physical reaction and most of us can remember times when we have felt very unwell. Even though the baked beans probably would not make him sick, he has been unable to confront or rationalize his fear. The sensation in our bodies that we call fear is a powerful emotion.

Fear can be a subconscious emotion. Indeed, until we feel that rush of adrenaline, the increased heartbeat, the closing down of non-essential bodily functions, the increased sensitivity as the hairs on the back of our neck stand up, we are unaware that these responses will occur. We do not go around thinking that we must remember to be scared today if something frightful occurs. The body simply reacts. Similarly, you do not remind yourself to have a smoke. It's just that you automatically feel a little anxious itch creeping up and you have a cigarette. A tiny little scared feeling that something is missing in your life catches up with you and you deal with it in the way you have always dealt with it, by lighting up.

The next time you have a spare ten minutes, I want you to go somewhere and smoke a cigarette and think about how you feel after you finish it. Do you feel the need to smoke another cigarette immediately? Probably not. Now close your eyes and, if you can, think of something from your childhood that frightened you until you feel a slight sense of reaction in your body. If you can make yourself a little uncomfortable in this way or, even better, frightened, the thought of having another cigarette becomes much more desirable, even though you have just put one out.

When smokers are nervous or scared, their emotions are naturally heightened and they turn to a cigarette. It may even be tempting to chain-smoke, but smoking those extra cigarettes does not in any way deal with the anxious situation. It simply compounds it. Fear is not the only reason for smoking. Indeed, when you are in a very comfortable situation – with friends or at a dinner party – you may feel the need for a smoke.

In these situations you smoke in an attempt to continue the relaxed feeling. This may sound like a contradiction – you smoke because you are anxious, and you smoke to prevent being anxious – but it is not. One of the reasons why smokers tend to smoke more when they are socializing is because they feel comfortable in a relaxed situation and they do not want to ruin the mood. But the solution is wrong. If you really want someone to relax, you advise them to take big, deep, slow breaths of fresh air, not quick, successive breaths of poisonous smoke. Smokers mistakenly think that they are relaxing simply because the brain is suffering, or about to suffer, a chemical withdrawal of a substance that it has been wrongly taught to associate with pleasure.

In fact, now you are going to stop smoking, you will feel more calm, complete and relaxed than you have in a long time. Getting back some control over your body is going to make you feel very good indeed. All your brain has to do is to see cigarettes for what they really are – a product that makes you feel uncomfortable, damages your health and can even kill you.

Key point

Give your mind the right answers and you will get the right reactions. Without the nicotine in your system, your old nicotine brain has nothing to hold on to.

Imagine this

This exercise can be useful to update your smoking brain and to deal with situations where you think you might struggle. The basis of this exercise is that if you can see/imagine it, then you can believe it.

As an example I have chosen a situation from my childhood between the ages of nine and 12 that I strongly associate with smoking. There was a real sense of daring adventure for me in climbing out onto the garage roof at night as I could watch everyone walking by and no one knew that I was there. I was not allowed out there and the whole operation was covert as there were consequences if I got caught. Even though the smoking part only took five minutes, I would stay out much longer and if a light came on in the window next to the garage I had perfected the 10ft drop by jumping onto the grass with a judo roll to break the fall, then running round the back of the house, in through the back door and straight into the bathroom to de-smoke myself. We smokers often have a strong connection to our youth in relation to smoking. We may have seen ourselves as pioneers and rebels – cool, sophisticated, tough, mature, adventurous, daring. The problem is that we connected these things with smoking, when, if you think about it, smoking made very little difference to the sense of adventure. For me, climbing onto the roof in secret, spying on passers-by and launching myself onto the grass or shinning down the drainpipe was the real adventure. Missing classes at school and sneaking across the playing fields with your boyfriend/girlfriend was the rebellious act, not the smoking; or hanging out with the cool kids at the back of the bus with your head half out of the window taking it turns to smoke a butt. I think you get the idea. Breaking the association is the key to living life contentedly and satisfied as a non-smoker. Now that you know the truth you can counter the trick that smoking has played on you.

So let me give that experience two scenarios. One is of my being anxious and empty, feeling a bit sick from the poison I am putting in my lungs and having to go out on the roof because I am weak and a young addict. The other is of the smoke-free kid who is somewhere between James Bond and Indiana Jones, strong, tough and adventurous and a bit of a rebel, free to do whatever I choose.

Now I close my eyes and visualize the first situation and wait until I can picture and feel the scenario. When I have done that I visualize the second situation. Then I repeat the exercise again and again until I start to notice a difference. The difference you are looking for is when it becomes much easier to see the new, positive, updated situation, but much harder to visualize the old negative scenario. Generally it takes between five and ten times, but keep going until you see a definite change.

Now you have got the idea, give it a go. Maybe pick more current situations, like when you think you are having the most desirable smoke, or when you imagine it hardest not to have a cigarette. For me, it would be sitting out in the back garden in the sunshine with a beer and watching the trees sway in the gentle breeze, or getting out onto the beach with a hot chocolate on a winter's day after surfing and watching the waves crash in. Neither of those situations is made better because of a cigarette, in fact completely the opposite. Indeed, these events are now more enjoyable because I have lost the feelings of anxiousness and emptiness that precede and follow a cigarette and I can enjoy the events for what they are.

Solution 12

By updating your faulty smoking brain, you are living a more honest experience.

13

Read the pack

Smoking kills

Cigarettes are the only product on sale that, if used as intended, will probably cause your premature death. You don't have to take my word for it; it says so on the pack. There are many other products that are poisonous, like detergents or fuels, but they are not designed to be consumed and finish you off. I mentioned this to someone the other day and he replied that an idiot or drunken driver behind the wheel of a car could be a more lethal weapon. My answer to that is that if used carefully or properly a car will not cause premature death. With cigarettes, no matter how careful you are, their constant use will bring about an earlier death and greatly reduce your quality of life, especially in the mid to later years.

At this point somebody usually says: 'My great auntie Edna smoked until she was 89 and she was always good for a laugh at Christmas and used to let me filch her smokes.' Well, my great auntie Phyllis was always a livewire at social events and she smoked to her dying day at the good old age of 83. A good friend of mine choked his way to death at the good old age of 53. I remember seeing him just before he passed away; he was so weak that he could barely lift his head, but he could just about lift a cigarette to his mouth to start him choking. When he was 12 years younger, he was the toughest person I knew. As for my great auntie Phyllis, her hands used to shake so much when she was trying to light her cigarette that she would often burn the front of her hair. In the last five years of her life the doctor said it was a close call as to whether she had her legs amputated and perhaps lived a little longer, or whether the clogged arteries caused by smoking would kill her. She opted for the quicker death with legs rather than the slow one without. Her sister, of a very similar build, recently celebrated her 92nd birthday at the Savoy Hotel in London. She stayed on the dance floor all night and danced with everyone in her family. In our family we all hope that we have our grandmother's genes, and I am also hoping that I have her great legs.

Some of my work as a fitness coach involves doing remedial exercises in a physiotherapy clinic, helping people to get more out of their bodies for longer. One smoker patient there recently

CIGARETTES CAN BE SUCH
A USEFUL CRUTCH

had a chest X-ray as part of a health check. The good news, as she delighted in telling us, was that she had a healthy chest, as strong as an ox, even though she smoked. The bad news was that although her lungs were feeling great the hospital had referred her to the clinic because she found it very difficult to walk and needed manipulation on her legs. After a while she did explain that her physician had told her she was probably going to lose at least one of her legs, and if she carried on smoking it was going to happen sooner rather than later.

It is interesting that we human beings often emphasize the positive dimensions of our lives when we are talking to others, as we do not want people to focus on our weaknesses. But the more honest we are about understanding our mistakes and faults the sooner we can learn and move forward. The sooner we stop lying to ourselves about our failings, the sooner our lives will become great. Otherwise, we just keep making the same mistake again and again. Ignorance is not bliss; it is simply a life lived without understanding!

In the UK in the mid 2000s there was a very graphic anti-smoking advertising campaign. It portrayed smoking cigarettes oozing the fatty deposits that build up in our arteries as we smoke. Instead of ash at the end of a burning cigarette there was the sticky, dribbling gunge that can be found in a smoker's clogged-up arteries. This was a well thought-out campaign. Non-smokers were disgusted by the adverts, which made them feel unwell. Smokers, on the other hand, tend to switch off their minds, and perhaps even their TV sets, as they reach for a comforting smoke. They reassure themselves that it will not happen to them, because currently they feel fine and, should they not, at that point they will stop smoking before anything serious happens. If someone confronts them with comments about adverts such as those, they will probably have a range of responses: for example, it is all hype; you can get clogged arteries from a bad diet; my great, great auntie twice removed on my mother's side smoked non-filter cigarettes for years and lived until she was 90. Another peach of a comment you get from smokers is 'If it was not for the taxes the government gets from us smokers there would not be a health service'. I shall not bore you with the figures here – they appear in another chapter – but I can assure you that that response simply does not add up.

I really wish that these horrible things were not going to happen if you carry on smoking. I wish that you could carry on smoking, thinking you enjoyed it and with no fear of ill-health. But I have to tell you that the odds are heavily stacked against you. Lung cancer, the illness most commonly associated with smoking, is a deadly disease, and 90 per cent of lung-cancer sufferers are smokers. Once you are diagnosed with lung cancer, the chances of survival are not high. My aim here is not to frighten. Instead I want you to get angry with the creatures who supplied you with the cigarettes in the first place. The people who purposely targeted you through trickery and false advertising to make you take up smoking. Those people who will not give a toss when you die as long as you smoke their brand until your dying day and do not file a lawsuit against them.

I would rather go blind and have a saggy bottom

I have to be honest with you; I have never seen the words 'Smoking Can Make You Go Blind And Give You A Drooping Backside' written on the side of a cigarette pack. Maybe because there is not enough room on the pack, or the government agencies feel that it is not hard-hitting enough. Unfortunately, though, the warnings are very true, but luckily neither of those ailments is as painful as suffocating from the dysfunction of your lungs.

The relationship between smoking and blindness has been proved by the AMD Alliance. AMD stands for age-related macular degeneration, which can result in irreversible loss of central vision and blindness. Pooled information gathered from three studies shows that smokers are three to four times more likely to suffer from blindness than non-smokers. At present in England there are an estimated 54,000 people suffering from AMD as a result of smoking. Again, I do not want you to panic, so I shall console you with the fact that the chances of dying from lung cancer are much higher.

After hearing that, the thought of suffering from a saggy bottom or saggy breasts is not really going to shock you into stopping smoking, especially if you are a man. At this point, you may feel free to breathe a sigh of relief or take another suck on that cigarette. Unfortunately, if you are a man it will make other parts of your body go saggy, as smoking hardens the arteries and clogs the flow of blood to your skin and extremities. Whatever age you are, smoking ages your body and skin prematurely by decreasing the flow of fresh oxygenated blood around your body, therefore making your skin lose its firmness and elasticity.

As I said at the beginning of this chapter, 'SMOKING KILLS' is written in big letters on packs of cigarettes. I think a better slogan would be 'Smoking is destroying you on your way to an early death'. When you go to the supermarket to buy food or when you pop to the shop to buy sweets, how many items of food would you buy if the slogan on the pack said 'This product kills'?

Health-wise, the great thing to remember is that the sooner you stop smoking, the sooner the odds start to stack up in your favour. The sooner you stop, the sooner you will feel more in control of your life and not dictated to by a multi-billion dollar corporation that has been screwing you for years with its conning product.

Solution 13

We all have to go sometime, but how you live your life determines how happy you are when you die.

14

I could get run over by a bus tomorrow

One of the arguments that smokers use is that there are many things more dangerous than smoking. Before I start giving examples that will refute this incorrect thought pattern, let's get one thing clear. If you carry on smoking for the rest of your life and are lucky enough to avoid all those big buses, you will die prematurely from some horrible, smoking-related disease. Now we all know what smokers are trying to say – life is short and you must do the things in life that make it more enjoyable. That argument does not hold because in reality you do not enjoy smoking and the slave it makes of you. This is one of the main reasons why you want to stop.

Many people enjoy the exhilarating effects of dangerous or contact sports. Take a sport like motor racing. Some people drive at high speeds, risking their lives for the buzz of adrenaline and sense of achievement that they get from competing and sometimes winning. Others get their kicks from cycling or skiing down a mountain with only their precision skills and athleticism to keep them from crashing. Even playing tennis or football holds some risk of injury, but all would argue that it is a risk worth taking. We all take calculated risks about the outcome and actions in our lives, from driving in icy conditions to where we fly to on holiday. With all these different actions there is an outcome that we want and we are willing to venture forward to get it.

The biggest risk that I take is going out in big surf. To some that may not seem scary but when I am out in big surf I know that there is some danger to my life. One of the most exciting experiences I have had was surfing a wave that was doubled over my head with a face of about 15 feet. In my own little way I am quite proud of myself and I even have photos of that day showing me on some of those waves. I do not have photos of myself smoking which I look at and say, yes, that was a good smoking day, well worth every drag on my cigarette. As a smoker I never felt the need to hang a pack of smokes on the wall and look at it with fond memories, thinking that it was a dangerous pastime but how lucky I was to have smoking in my life. You could be tempted to nail your last pack of cigarettes to the wall so you can pat yourself on the back and tell yourself how good you feel that you do not have to do that anymore.

When you watch an adventure or horror movie, you may see the hero about to enter a dangerous situation in search of treasure. He believes that behind the next door is the golden treasure but you and the rest of the audience know that a big rock is about to fall on him and a large, three-headed monster is waiting to eat up his remains. You even find yourself shouting at the screen in the vain hope that he can hear you trying to warn of the obvious doom that is about to befall.

If that does not strike a chord, how about reading a book in which the heroine is about to marry the man of her dreams but unknown to her she is about to make the biggest mistake in her life. Her gorgeous husband-to-be is actually having an affair with her mother, has designs on her sister and is plotting to bump her off in some accident and steal her money so he can elope with her father! Everyone else is aware of the mistake she is about to make, but in spite of her beloved's murky past she is sure it is going to work this time. The heroine is willing to risk everything for the chance of true happiness. The adventurer is willing to take his chance with the rock and monster to get the treasure.

Risk versus reward

These two characters are taking a big risk but for them there is the slight chance of some reward, in one case the possibility of love and in the other the lure of fame and wealth. To me it seems like a risk worth taking if that was what you really wanted. If you choose an action, you accept the consequences that go with it. You are not going to choose to step out in front of a bus, because where would the benefit be in that? You might be unlucky and happen to be standing in the wrong place and a lorry accidentally squashes your foot, but you did not purposely put yourself in harm's way. After you smoked your first few cigarettes you did not think, 'This is fantastic! I hope that I can do this for the rest of my life'. It is not your fault that you started smoking. No one was telling you all the facts about smoking when you first lit up, so you were not to blame when it came to smoking another and another and so on. The chemicals in your body made your brain choose for you to carry on smoking without your consent. There is no reward

WITH BUSES
YOU NEVER KNOW.
WITH SMOKING
IT'S A SURE THING.

from smoking, only relief. The best sensation you can get from smoking is realizing that you do not have to do it any longer.

If you want to use the 'I could get run over by a bus' excuse about your smoking, then what you should say is that smoking is like standing in front of a bus that is still some distance away and if you do not get out of the bus lane soon, then the bus will definitely run you over. That would be a more accurate analogy of the situation you are in as a smoker.

Now that you know there is no reward, only relief, you cannot go on kidding yourself that smoking is a pleasure that you are willing to risk. With smoking it is all risk and no reward.

Solution 14

If you carry on smoking, you are already standing in front of a bus; it's just not here yet.

15

Children and smoking

Today, education about drugs and addictive substances is more widespread than ever before. It is now commonplace for the police or drugs prevention organizations to go into schools and talk about the effects of drugs and the damage they can do. I include nicotine with other hard drugs because many people believe that if nicotine had first appeared in modern times, it would be classified as a class C drug. Many schools also have a smoke-testing machine that shows children how tar deposits from inhaling tobacco smoke stain a thin white cloth. The cloth is meant to resemble your soft, pink lungs and shows the build-up of black tar deposits that form on your lungs when you smoke. Thankfully, smoking advertising is much reduced and the health information young people receive is better than ever. But are these changes sufficient to prevent children from trying smoking?

No sane person would ever recommend that a young person should start smoking. In fact no one would recommend smoking to anyone. Think about how you would try to entice someone to take up smoking. How would you start?

'Go on, young Johnny, have one of these. They taste fantastic and they are guaranteed to kill you at least 15 years prematurely, especially if you can smoke 30 a day by the time you are ten!'

'How would you like to take up this delightful pastime that is just like burning five pound notes every day, has no benefit to it (except for tobacco companies) and, if you try really hard at it, you might be able to have one of your legs amputated as a result of clogged arteries.'

'It makes you stink; it decreases your sex drive; it poisons you and your unborn child; it ages your skin prematurely. It can upset your digestive system and does not make you lose weight. All for under a tenner a pack; how can you resist it?'

I'm sure you can easily make up your own adverts without my help, but not one of them would make you want to promote smoking to anyone, especially children.

Unfortunately, by the time we see kids smoking on the streets they have probably been smoking for some time and it's too late to put them off with scare tactics. Try telling a teenager that he or she is going to spend the last 15 years of their life breathing out of an oxygen tank because one of their lungs has packed up. The reply would probably be, 'Sod off, you old duffer', or 'If getting older means I'll end up like you then I'll be glad if I am dead by 30'.

When I was growing up I felt that smoking was an exciting thing to do, and after a while I thought I actually enjoyed it. My friends and I would go off somewhere to do something that was fun and when we got there we would have a cigarette. Sometimes the adventure was having a cigarette or trying to get cigarettes without getting into trouble. On many occasions my good friend Darren and I would climb up a tree in my front garden and smoke a couple of cigarettes while we watched the adults walk past, oblivious to the adventure unfolding above them. On more

than one occasion the excitement was enhanced when someone like my mother ventured out onto the drive and we could see her but she could not see us blowing smoke rings in her direction.

'No child of mine would get away with that,' I hear you say, 'or have that flagrant disregard for the discipline that I maintain in my household.' Well, kids are smarter than you think! If they want to do something without their parents finding out, they will find a way of doing it. As children, we would arm ourselves with all the equipment we needed to avoid being found out or getting caught. We would carry mints, toothpaste, breath sprays, even tissue paper to stop the matches rattling. If we weren't able to wash our hands before we got home, we could identify the herbs and plants to rub on our hands to remove the smell of cigarettes. If there was a chance of being searched before getting to your bedroom, there were always hiding places for the cigarettes outside the house, and there was always the last resort of lying and denying all knowledge. This could be anything from 'I was sitting next to a heavy smoker at the bus stop' to 'I am minding these cigarettes for a friend who asked me to look after them as it would help him to cut down his smoking'. OK, so not all of my excuses worked!

When I got caught smoking I was normally in real trouble. I would not be allowed out for a month (that meant I would have to climb out onto the garage roof for a cigarette, which was even more exciting). I would have my pocket money taken away (which was a test of who your friends were as they would supply you with the illegal contraband until your finances resumed). I would normally get beaten up by my older brother because he was trying to instil the idea that smoking was bad for me, and a stupid thing to do. To which I would reply, 'You must just be more stupid than me because you're older than I am and you still do it'. That's normally when the fighting would start. The benefit of being beaten up by my older brother was that I did not feel so guilty about stealing his cigarettes. My eldest brother finally stopped smoking at 41 – which was fantastic news. I wish I could say that I played a part in that but I learned at an early age you cannot force your brother to do something that he thinks he does not want to do. Especially when the person relaying the message is doing the one thing they are telling you not to do.

Obviously I do not have all the answers when it comes to getting children and teenagers to do as they are told all of the time. If I did I would not be writing self-help books; I would probably be ruler of the universe. However, as a smoker you are going to find it very hard to get the no-smoking message across to your kids when you're having to pause at regular intervals to take an extra large drag (you know that extra hard sucking sound) while explaining that smoking is a mug's game and is not good for them. What might work better is when you're a little older and you have to carry round an oxygen bottle in order to breathe; then you can tell them that perhaps smoking is not such a good idea to some effect.

Parents need to be clear about why there is no point to smoking. Portray smoking as the evil thing that it is; ask your children to tell you of all the reasons why they should not smoke. If you think bribing them will help, then do it. Even if you suspect them of smoking, do not just shout at them; shout very, very loudly if you think it will work, then quietly sit down with them and shout some more. Remember, though, that your job as their parent is to help them stop their addiction. You know how easy it is to become addicted to smoking, but luckily you now have all the answers and you can be ready with your replies to their excuses. You know your children and you know what motivates them. Think of ways to include their understanding of life and how smoking will affect them, in the short term as well as the long term. If there has been a death in the family – whether a family member or a pet – use the emotion that they felt in that situation to make them realize what it is like to lose someone and how we all want to enjoy life for as long as possible. Ask them to think of all the great times you have had together and how smoking was never part of it. Use scare tactics. Ground them for two months; take away their income. If you can afford it, promise them a car for their 17th birthday. If you can't afford it, promise that if they do not stop you will walk them to school or work every day until they are 18 and that you will give them a big kiss in front of all their friends. Whatever you do, do something! Do not let them carry on without understanding why they do it. As they get older they will understand and thank you for it.

I have heard from many couples that their children were instrumental in persuading them to stop smoking. Children learn about the dangers of smoking at school. Some share this information with their parents – to good effect. A frightened child who fears for his or her parents' health can be a powerful motivator. So, as you would expect, the parents make the effort to quit smoking. Unfortunately, neither child nor parent is risk-free. As children grow into teenagers, they are subjected to a range of new pressures to begin smoking themselves.

Recent research shows that parents who smoke in front of their children may do more harm than they realize. Besides the obvious dangers of the bad example they set, there is some evidence that smoking parents are priming their children to become smokers in later life. This is not just because they copy their parents, but may stem from the children acquiring an early taste for nicotine. A Montreal study followed 200 children from the age of nine and measured the levels of cotinine in their saliva. Cotinine is a by-product which is produced in our bodies by the absorption of nicotine. At age nine, although cotinine levels varied considerably, only one child was deemed to be a smoker. By age 13, 44 per cent of the children were smokers. The researchers found that saliva cotinine levels at age nine were a good predictor of who would be smoking by age 13. This was a small-scale study. The need for more research in this area is clear.

As an adult smoker you may have some understanding of why you feel the need for a smoke. Children do not understand why they crave the things they do; they just put the thing that fits and relieves the desire in their mouths. As a smoker, you are leading your children by the hand into smoking their first and possibly their 50,000th cigarette.

Remember, smoking is like hitting yourself in the face all day long only to relieve the pain for five minutes when you have a smoke; then you go back to hitting yourself just so you can feel comfortable later when you again stop for another five minutes. That is how a pointless addiction like smoking works. When you're clear that there is no point to smoking, it will be much easier to convey that message to children, both yours and others.

If you are a smoker, your children are not going to believe you when you tell them that smoking is bad for their health. Even packs displaying the warning 'SMOKING KILLS' are not much of a deterrent. Any child, as well as any rational smoker, can answer that with, 'Well, I've seen other people smoking and they are still alive'. Everyone has a relative – be it an aunt or a grandfather – who lived to 90 and still smoked. These relatives may have lost all feeling in their legs due to clogged arteries but they were still alive. You need to get across an understanding of addiction, and how smoking is a trap designed to waste your life at the expense of your health. The longer you smoke, the longer you are wasting your life, your health and your money.

Chapter 22 is aimed at young smokers. It says the same thing as the rest of the book, but in a condensed version. Its aim is to encourage younger people to read the rest of the book. I do not know exactly what motivates your child, but I do know that scare tactics do not work once children reach a certain age. From an early age I knew that I did not want to smoke, but I never understood why I could not stop. I did everything else I ever wanted to, but I could not work out what kept drawing me back to smoking.

As I am sure you know, your children need your understanding and encouragement in whatever they do. If you think that they are smoking from an early age, then the sooner you do something positive about it the easier it is going to be for them – and you. Remember that once you have started smoking, you are a drug addict. Fortunately, nicotine is not the worst drug in the world but it is certainly a drug. Children and young people do not want to smoke, it just happens; first one and then another and another. Once you are hooked you will always defend your addiction, especially if it is a secret among friends. As an adult smoker, you have always defended smoking with your excuses and failure to understand the nature of the nicotine beast. Just as you have defended your smoking, so will your children defend theirs.

Solution 15

No one, especially children, thinks that they will be the ones to die from smoking, but no one likes being fooled at the expense of their health, money and freedom of choice.

16

Cutting back

All smokers envy those people who only seem to smoke a few chosen cigarettes a day. We tell ourselves if we could only smoke the three most enjoyable cigarettes out of the day, then everything would be rosy in our world of smoking. Some smokers wait until they get to work before they light up or until their first cup of coffee at work; some may even wait until after their evening meal or their first glass of wine.

You may know of people who limit their intake to one after every meal – breakfast, lunch and dinner – but many of these smokers tend to be liars, not just to their friends but also to themselves. They will gladly tell everyone that they are in control of their smoking addiction by only smoking after meals. If you were to follow them around, though, you would find out that included in their meals are an elevenses, twelveses, a just-past-threeses, a quarter-past-threeses, an after eight, a late-night supper and, possibly, a midnight feast. Most people who cut back on smoking are either coming back from a failed attempt at giving up and working their way back to their regular intake, or attempting to half quit before they try to stop. You either smoke or you do not! There is no halfway house. One cigarette will always lead to another, and another and another.

If you stumble when you try to limit when you should or can smoke, you tend to fall flat on your face. The one thing you console yourself with after your failure is a heavy session of smoking, because you believe that you need it and life seems to be more content with it. Cutting back will make smoking seem more precious than ever, because you will be counting down the seconds to your next cigarette. As soon as you put that cigarette out the whole cycle starts again.

For those smokers who do manage to limit themselves to just a couple of cigarettes in the evening, you may want to ask, 'Why bother?'. If smoking is such an enjoyable thing to do, why limit it to just a couple in the evening? Why do you not have a couple in the morning, a couple in the afternoon and then a couple in the evening? Surely smoking only six cigarettes cannot be that bad for you.

Fear is the answer. If these part-time smokers started smoking more, it could lead to more and more. These smokers know the destructive nature of smoking; they think as long as they can keep it down to two a day they are in control and will not die of some horrible, smoking-related disease. What they are actually doing is living most of their days in torment. If you speak to one of these part-time smokers and ask them how many times they think about smoking during a day, it will be much more than your average smoker. They are living part of their day tormented by the subtle withdrawal symptoms of smoking. When they see a smoker or smell cigarette smoke, their brain cannot help but say to them, 'We need to get some of that'. I believe it would be better to smoke 60 a day and die earlier, happy in the false belief that you smoked because you thought that you enjoyed it. Believing, indeed, that you were in control of your life and that you dictated your pleasure and enjoyment (it would not be true but it's a nice idea). The reality is that you torture yourself with a few chosen cigarettes and for the minutes that you smoke, you think you are in control.

As discussed earlier, rationing your smoking is like hitting yourself all day only to enjoy the ten minutes of pleasure when you stop hitting yourself. What torture! If a report came out tomorrow that told us that smoking was good for us and not addictive, these part-time smokers would smoke more than anyone else. In fact that report will never appear because, as you know, if they took out the addictive harmful chemicals in tobacco then they would be taking away the reason why you smoke.

One of the ways I tried to cut down on smoking was to try to limit my smoking to when I went out for a drink. I convinced myself that if I could confine my smoking to when I had the odd drink, I would be in control of smoking and I would choose when and where I smoked. Over a nine-year period, the two properties that I lived in were right next door to pubs. From one of the houses I could literally spit from the back garden into the pub's back garden, although I had to give up that filthy habit because the pub landlord said he would stop serving me.

So on the occasions when I was implementing the 'only smoke when I drink' technique, you would find me next door in the pub having a 'quick' drink. At one point over a period of three weeks I put on an extra ten pounds from all the beer I drank and spent an extra £200 on the booze, fruit machine and playing pool. As I was only going into the pub for a quick smoke, obviously, I had to go back to full-time smoking before I became a broke alcoholic. At the time I actually believed that I was winning the war on smoking because I was able to not smoke during the day and wait until later in the evening before I lit up. In my mind I felt that if I could cut back on the drinking a bit I would be in control of smoking. To any sane person looking at that situation it is obvious that I was never in control of my smoking addiction. Trying to cut back would just compound the fact that I was a smoker and that I needed to smoke to make me feel normal. The time when I would feel calm and complete was when I was smoking.

We all seem to know someone that we think has cracked the 'only smoking when they want to and when they are socializing' syndrome. I have a friend who I thought until recently had the self-discipline to smoke only when she wanted to. I would even purposely not mention this book to her because she was confident that she was in control of smoking and she dictated when she smoked. I felt that she had nothing to gain from me because she did not need or want any help. Of the many thousand smokers I have talked to there have been a few like this but I am mentioning this lady because many people who met her would be impressed with her mental and physical strength.

Alison is very fit and self-disciplined. She runs a pub with her new husband and still finds the time to teach over ten exercise classes a week and bring up her children. Not long ago, Alison told me she would be interested in reading this book and getting some advice about not wanting to smoke. I was pleased and a little surprised by what she later told me.

Alison and I share many friends who work in the health and fitness industry and I am sure that many of you, like me, would be amazed at how many of them smoke – very similar to the numbers of young doctors and nurses that you see smoking outside hospitals. At this point you must remember that anyone who falls into the trap of smoking can become a smoker, regardless of their profession. So when I go out with my healthy friends I make a point of not talking about some of the work that I do, as it can become boring talking about smoking all night. But most of these part-time heading back to full-time-again smokers can't resist telling me that they have got their smoking down to a controlled minimum. I never initiate these conversations; it must be that I have a discerning look on my face or maybe I look as if I am about to tell them off. Someone once told me that when you see something you do not like in a person's expression, it can be that it is actually you looking back at yourself. I shall leave it up to you to decide whether that is true or not.

Of all these would-be part-time smokers, Alison was the one who could have been telling the truth, whereas all the others I knew were always falling in and out of being heavy to light smokers. So while we were having a chat about smoking she explained to me that she had recently stopped going round to see certain friends because she found herself smoking every time she was with them. This was not just when going out in the evenings, but in the daytime as well. It turns out she had created a network of people that were good friends and she would almost subconsciously plan to see certain friends when she felt a greater need to smoke. Because Alison was a person who always considered herself in control of her smoking, she was becoming dismayed at how much she was smoking. She decided that to cut back on her smoking she would have to cut back on who she visited and which friends she went out with. Luckily, this uncomfortable situation did not last long because Alison knew that she did not want to smoke. Nowadays, Alison does not smoke any more. She can visit any friend she likes and she really does have control over smoking.

What you will come to realize is that the satisfaction you feel when you have a cigarette is the way every non-smoker feels all the time. As a smoker, the only time you feel it is when you are smoking. When you have stopped smoking you will feel that sensation of satisfaction all the time and you will not miss a thing.

Solution 16

You either smoke or you do not; smoke one cigarette and it leads to another and another and another, and so on.

Every so often your brain will say, 'I fancy having just one cigarette'; just remember that you do not want the other 50,000 cigarettes that go with it.

17

Free holidays every year

Every year the price of cigarettes goes up as the government increases the percentage of tax on each pack. The government's aim is to dissuade people from buying cigarettes, while the revenue raised is also useful for helping to fund health, social and other services. The policy works to some degree. As prices increase, some smokers do cut down and others consider giving up. The response of some UK smokers, however, is to travel abroad to stock up on duty-free cigarettes and other goods, or to buy the smuggled cigarettes that sell for about 60 to 70 per cent of the normal UK price.

The average price of a pack of cigarettes in the UK was £7.60 in 2012, while in the USA prices varied from less than $5 to over $12, depending on state taxes. The only way to get cigarettes more cheaply is to buy them duty-free abroad or find someone that smuggles them into the country. When most people think of smuggled cigarettes, they think of that friendly bloke who turns up at work with his black bag or the chatty lady you look for at the car boot sales who always has your favourite carton of cigarettes. But although it does not appear to be as threatening or to carry as high a penalty or risk as transporting heroin or people, cigarette smuggling is a billion-dollar business. Organized criminals bring tonnes of cigarettes into countries and so evade paying duty or tax. The profit margins are particularly high in countries like the UK and Canada where there are heavy taxes on cigarettes.

Tobacco companies could never be seen to condone the evasion of paying tax on cigarettes. However, at the end of the day, why should they care who buys their product, as long as someone buys it? Smuggling greatly benefits the tobacco industry because it makes it easier for people to begin and to carry on smoking. If the price of cigarettes is low, they become more accessible to a wider range of people, including the young.

Some smokers won't buy duty-free cigarettes when they come back from holiday, because they do not like the idea of having over 200 cigarettes or ten pouches of tobacco in the house. You will know if you are one of these people. Every time you come back from holiday you think you are going to give up smoking.

You walk past all the shiny, big boxes of 200 cigarettes at the airport and you tell yourself that the reason you are not buying them is that you will give up long before you could smoke all of them. In your mind, all you need is a trusty pack in your pocket that will see you through to getting off the plane, the journey home and a bite to eat, with a couple of smokes spare for those extra cups of coffee or tea before you go to bed.

I do know one or two very disciplined people who have managed to quit on the plane home. But for most of us the odds are seriously stacked against this. When you go on holiday you tend to have a relaxing, fun, exciting and sometimes adventurous time. On the way back you think of ways that would make more of your life a holiday. If your holiday destination has been especially exciting you may even start planning how you could live there permanently. So generally when you are on holiday you are on a high. What happens to most of us when we return home? We go straight back to work. Unless you have the most fantastic job in the world this can be a rather depressing time. Especially if you live in England and you have returned from three weeks in the tropics to rain, the M25 motorway and London congestion charging. The depressed feeling may be compounded when you get back to work and find that no one has been covering your job while you were away and your work partner has decided to head off on her four-week trip to Australia. Aaargh!

At this exact moment that carton of 200 duty-free cigarettes would be very handy to see you through the next few days. Trying to stop using only your willpower is never going to be an enjoyable experience, but trying to give up using willpower alone immediately after a holiday borders on the suicidal. You would probably end up reconfirming to your nicotine brain that cigarettes are an essential part of your make-up and you are more depressed without them, so therefore you must smoke. Thankfully, by reading this book, you are starting to realize that cigarettes are actually what make you more depressed at times when you are not at your best. Very few people relish the thought of going back to work after a fantastic holiday and life can seem a little dull on your return. Well, cheer up,

because things in the future are going to get a lot better, and
your next holiday could be much sooner than you think.

The average smoker smokes 15 cigarettes a day. Allowing for
a few handouts, some extra-long phone calls and the amount
you smoke when you go out or at the weekend, you can easily
see that the average smoker gets through a pack a day. A quick
calculation tells me that each year you are blowing £2,774 on
something that you really hate doing. Even if you only smoke
half that number or get your cigarettes from a cheap source, it's
still around £1,500 a year. When you realize that you would be
better off if you took that £2,774 and threw it down the toilet
or set it on fire, it all becomes rather disconcerting. I have come
across desperate smokers who argue that they would still pay
the money as long as they did not have to smoke any more.
The great realization is that you do not have to do that, and the
money you save can either be used more wisely or blown on
a fantastic holiday. Personally, I believe that you should treat
yourself whenever possible, and failing that, treat someone you
love or care for, or someone who needs it more than you do.

The saving of money from not smoking is an argument in itself
for quitting smoking, but it is even more enticing to think about

what you could do with the extra cash. If you are a person who sees the glass as half full rather than half empty, you could view the amount of money saved as double the actual saving when you allow for potential future tax increases and your heavier smoking in the future. You do not need smoking in your life and why should you pay for it in more ways than one?

Even if £2,774 is a drop in the ocean to you, why not save that money and give it to a favourite charity? Three thousand pounds could feed and support more than one starving family in Africa for a year, so not only would you be saving your own life, but you would also be making a difference to many others. That must make you feel good, and the taste left in your mouth would be a lot sweeter than that of a stinking cigarette.

Solution 17

The biggest saving is your sanity from the madness of smoking, but the money also comes in handy.

18

Extra stress

As smokers, we believe that smoking is essential to our resilience; we feel that as long as we have our cigarettes we can get through the strains and stresses of life. You can recall times when you felt under pressure or went through some challenging ordeal and everything was all right in the end because you highlighted the event with a cigarette. If I told you that you had to take a general knowledge exam tomorrow and it was an oral test in front of all the people you work with, you would probably be nervous. Would you remember the event because of what you did, or would you remember the cigarette that you smoked afterwards? You have just had a massive argument with your partner. Do you remember the smoke you had to go out and have, or do you remember the shouting? You go to the bank and find that the last few cheques you have paid in are not there? When you get outside the bank and light up that cigarette, does the problem go away?

The only thing that goes away when you have that smoke is the annoying, nagging sensation of the need for some nicotine. That nagging sensation could also be called stress. So besides the hassle of the original problem of the exam, the argument or the lost cheques, you have the added stress of not getting your nicotine while dealing with it. You have to wait until you get outside before you can relieve that part of the problem. What makes matters worse is that instead of getting on and dealing with the stressful situation, you waste time having a smoke. Smoking causes you stress; it is not the helper that you have built it up to be. These events and any other stressful situations you can imagine are not resolved by having a cigarette. You highlight all the events in your life with a cigarette – whether it is getting a job promotion, being dumped, losing a loved one, getting out of bed, going to the toilet, having the first glass of wine and the second and the third.

Stress is a natural part of life; we need a certain amount of it in our lives to get us going. Suppose you never got concerned about anything or never had to deal with a problem? Imagine if all decisions were made for you and all you had to do was turn up and not think. Think about what life would be like if you never had to get somewhere or work out your own or someone else's problem. How would life be if you always stayed well within your comfort zone and never stood up for anything you thought was right, or never pushed yourself to make that extra effort or deal with that awkward situation? You would be a mindless slave, not living your life but just passing through life on your way to death. A bit of natural stress is a good thing, but believing that smoking relieves it could not be further from the truth.

As a smoker, the whole time you are not smoking there is a little voice in your head saying 'You need to have a smoke'. A little later the voice says more loudly, 'You really should have a cigarette'. Time goes by and the voice is screaming, 'The time is now and I am not prepared to wait. GO NOW AND SMOKE AND I WILL NOT SHOUT AT YOU'. Another way of experiencing a similar sensation is to put a young child in the back of a car and tell him or her as you start the journey that you are nearly there. Then drive to somewhere far away and see what happens. It will not be long before you hear relentlessly from the back seat, 'Are we there yet, are we there yet, are we there yet, are we there yet, are we there yet, are we there yet, are we there yet?'. You may be able to distract the child for the rest of the journey, but as a smoker you have to light up to relieve that pain and as soon as you put out that cigarette the pressure starts to build again. When you stop smoking, the pain of wanting to smoke soon goes away, so every day you feel better until the noise of 'Are we there yet?' goes away forever.

If you feel that your life is too stressful you must make a change. Without making a change, the stress will continue. Ideals, words and dreams are a great way to start the process, but if you do not physically do something and act upon those ideas, then nothing will change. To relieve the stress of smoking, you must mentally and physically rid yourself of the idea that smoking was ever any use to you and gave you some benefit. Not doing what you want to be able to do is one of the most stressful situations in life. Not feeling free and being beholden to something you hate and detest is not the way you want to live and that is why you no longer want to be a smoker.

Boredom

Boredom is a state that arises when you are not doing what you want and you feel that time is being wasted, which also can be a cause of stress. It is sometimes argued that people smoke to relieve their boredom. If your life feels as if it is stuck in a rut and one of the few pleasures you have is to sit in front of the television with your favourite drink and relish every smoky drag on your cigarette, that to me sounds boring. Is work so boring that the only relief you get from it is when you pop outside for a smoke? While sitting in traffic, is the only relief from tired thoughts to be gained by lighting up your precious cigarette and flicking your ash out of the window? Is smoking one of your excuses for not moving on? Does it always seem easier to light up and watch the world go by? I know that smoking held me back from some of the achievements I wanted in my earlier life. Instead of having the extra energy to get on with things, it was always easier to light up and console myself that this did not matter as long as I could have my little fix. I hate to say it, but if your life is boring it is probably because you have become a boring person and you need to change that. Smoking gives you an excuse to do less and it holds you in its own little trap.

The extra confidence and extra energy you have when you stop smoking will encourage you to get more out of your life. When you realize that you have regained control of your body, it is easier to get on with what you want to do. Once you stop making excuses for smoking, it becomes easier to stop making excuses about other areas of your life. As a human being, you have the ability to bring pleasure, happiness, love, generosity, understanding and joy to any room you walk into. It seems an absolute waste of your life to be bored, just as much as it is a waste of your life to smoke. I feel that if there was more room on a cigarette pack, they should put a warning that says, 'MAY LEAD TO WASTEFUL DISTRACTION IN LIVING YOUR LIFE'.

Solution 18

When you are stressed by a particular situation, you need to do something to make that situation change and move forward. Smoking just adds more discomfort to an already uncomfortable situation.

19

A bit of background

This chapter explains how smoking began and developed. It shows that in historical terms, smoking is a comparatively recent invention. It also shows that in the past 50 years overwhelming scientific evidence as to its harmful effects means that in many countries, including the UK and USA, smokers are now giving up. History, then, is on your side.

In 1931, Count Corti concluded his famous book *A History of Smoking* with a chapter entitled 'The Final Triumph of Smoking'. Corti was convinced that governments could never reverse the spread of smoking. He maintained that while in the USA it had been possible to contain and even prohibit the consumption of alcohol, any government that tried to prohibit smoking would be swept out of office. But Corti was wrong. In some countries the tide of smoking history has been dramatically reversed as the result of government actions.

American origins

According to experts, the tobacco plant began to grow on the American continent about 8,000 years ago. Native Americans inhaled, chewed and smoked tobacco, and these practices are shown in the art of the Maya people who lived in central America. By AD 1000 the habit had spread north and south through the Americas. Some Maya moved as far as the Mississippi valley, while a piece of pottery showing a Maya smoking a 'cigar' of tobacco leaves tied with string has been found in Guatemala. Tobacco was believed to have magical and healing powers, and tobacco gourds were worn by midwives as a badge of office. Tobacco was also burned in sacrifices to the gods.

The importance of tobacco was such that when Columbus landed on San Salvador in the Americas in 1492, he recorded that among the important gifts presented by the native Arawaks were 'certain dried leaves which gave off a distinct fragrance'. Columbus wisely threw them away.

Columbus then moved on to Cuba where two members of his expedition, Luis de Torres and Rodrigo de Jerez, saw people smoking cigars made of dried tobacco wrapped in palm or maize.

Jerez adopted the habit but in 1493, after he was bold enough to smoke in public following his return to Spain, he was thrown into prison for three years by the Inquisition. Smoking, however, soon caught on and the Spanish government realized that tobacco might become its most profitable import from the New World. Seville became the centre for cigar production in Europe and it is probable that in Seville tobacco fragments from used cigars were rolled in scraps of paper to make the first European cigarettes (known as *papaletes*).

The English sea captains Sir John Hawkins and Sir Francis Drake and their crews probably introduced smoking to England. Sir Walter Raleigh, who organized several expeditions to America, planted tobacco and potatoes on his estate at Youghal in Ireland, and popularized smoking at the court of Queen Elizabeth I, even persuading the queen herself to give it a try. The colony of Virginia, which was to become so strongly identified with tobacco, was named for the queen. At first, Elizabeth's successor, King James I, strongly opposed smoking and in 1604 published a book entitled *A Counterblast to Tobacco*. Smoking was described as 'an invention of Satan' and was banned from London taverns, while the import tax on tobacco was greatly increased. Ten years later, as the potential for revenue generation became clear, the importation of tobacco became a royal monopoly. In 1619 the London clay-pipe makers were incorporated into a chartered body. Their coat of arms included both a pipe and a roll of tobacco. Another development was to powder and scent tobacco and inhale it through the nostrils in the form of snuff. King Charles II and his courtiers were credited with bringing this aristocratic practice to Britain from France when the monarchy was restored in 1660. In the 18th century, Queen Charlotte, the wife of King George III, was so addicted that she was generally known as 'snuffy Charlotte'.

Tobacco spreads

During the 16th and 17th centuries smoking spread around the world. Europeans established tobacco plantations in the Americas and in trading posts in other parts of the world.

Dutch and Portuguese traders carried the new habit as far as Japan, where tobacco seeds were sometimes used as payment for lodging and other services.

The plant was also grown in Europe. One of the pioneers was Jean Nicot, a Frenchman who, in 1559, had seen tobacco plants growing in Lisbon, where the leaves were used to cure wounds and ulcers. On his return to France, Nicot did his best to popularize the healing powers of tobacco. His name is perpetuated in *Nicotiana*, the botanical name first given to the tobacco plant in 1570, and in 'nicotine', the essence of the plant, which was isolated in the early 19th century.

Tobacco became central to the economy of some American colonies. In 1611 John Rolfe planted some tobacco seeds in Virginia and in 1616 travelled to London with his wife, the dazzling Indian princess Pocahontas, to promote the new crop. In 1619 the first law passed by Virginia's assembly was that tobacco should not be sold for less than three shillings a pound. Indeed, tobacco became so important that it was widely used as currency. For example, in 1621, 60 prospective wives who arrived in Virginia were sold for 150 lb of tobacco each (in 1619 the price had been only 120 lb).

Meanwhile, in other parts of the world, the authorities turned to ever more stringent punishments to stamp out smoking. The popes Clement VIII and Urban VIII threatened those who smoked in a holy place with excommunication. Tsar Alexei of Russia decreed two levels of punishment: whipping, a slit nose and lips and transportation to Siberia for a first offence, and execution for a second. Sultan Murad IV of Turkey was less considerate; those caught smoking were immediately executed. A similar fate awaited smokers in China.

At this time arguments against smoking, such as the risk of starting a fire and the danger to health, were very similar to those of today. In contrast, a number of spurious claims were made for the medical benefits of tobacco, for example, as a cure for toothache and cancer, while in 1665 smoking was made compulsory for the boys of Eton College as a means of warding off the great plague of that year.

Until the early part of the 20th century, smoking was almost an exclusively male activity and the two main methods were the pipe and the cigar. When King Edward VII succeeded his mother, Queen Victoria, in 1901, he entered the drawing room in Buckingham Palace cigar in hand, and famously informed the assembled company, 'Gentlemen, you may smoke'. Smoking jackets and hats became fashionable, and in Britain it became customary for gentlemen to end a meal with a cigar and a glass (or more) of brandy or port while the ladies withdrew.

Cigarettes and war

The cigarette also began in a masculine context and the origins of the modern cigarette are often traced to wartime events. It is generally believed that the first paper-rolled cigarettes were made by Egyptian soldiers when fighting the Turks in 1832. The story goes that an Egyptian gunner and his crew had improved the efficiency of their rate of fire by rolling gunpowder in paper tubes. Rewarded with tobacco (Mehemet Ali, the ruler of Egypt, had previously been a tobacco dealer) but lacking any pipes with which to smoke it, the soldiers wrapped the tobacco in paper. The invention spread among the armies of both sides, and during the Crimean War (1853–6) British soldiers were introduced to cigarettes by their Turkish allies. In 1854, the London tobacconist Philip Morris, who for some years had been selling Turkish hand-rolled cigarettes, began producing his own. Two years later, a Crimean War veteran, Robert Gloag, opened the first cigarette factory, in Walworth, south London.

During the American Civil War (1861–5), the armies of both sides were given chewing tobacco along with other rations. The commander of the Southern forces, Robert E. Lee, was a non-smoker, but his main adversary, the Northern general Ulysses S. Grant, was a cigar addict. When Grant captured Fort Donelson in 1862, well-wishers from all over the North sent him a gift of 11,000 cigars. The First World War (1914–18) saw cigarettes distributed to troops on both sides as a means of coping with stress, and cigarettes became known as the 'soldier's smoke'. Indeed, the American general John Joseph Pershing, a former schoolteacher who commanded the

American Expeditionary Force in Europe, advised, 'You ask what we need to win this war; I answer tobacco, as much as bullets'. After the war the tobacco companies not only kept their newly acquired male smokers but also made a determined effort to promote cigarette smoking among women.

Tobacco advertising

Tobacco advertising has a long history, and from the 16th century onwards producers and retailers used a variety of methods to draw attention to their products. In the 1880s the Duke firm of Durham, North Carolina installed cigarette machines, invented by James Bonsack, which could produce 120,000 neatly packed cigarettes a day. 'Buck' Duke is credited with producing some of the first cigarette cards, but the practice was soon adopted by rival firms. Cigarette cards reached out to a wider public as smokers, and others, sought to collect complete sets of sportsmen, film stars and the like. Pictures were provided on one side of the card and brief biographies on the other. Successful advertising guaranteed huge profits for tobacco companies and by the mid-1920s, R. J. Reynolds' Camel, with its slogan of 'I'd Walk a Mile for a Camel', was by far the most popular cigarette brand in the USA, with over 40 per cent of the market.

In 1924, Philip Morris launched Marlboro specifically as a women's cigarette that was 'Mild as May'. Soon all the major tobacco companies were targeting female customers with the promise of more feminine cigarettes that would enhance the image of a modern independent woman, and employing film stars and models to promote their particular brands. For example, to the dismay of confectioners, Lucky Strike achieved great success with the slogan 'Reach for a Lucky instead of a Sweet'. For the next 40 years tobacco advertising and successful role models were everywhere to be seen. Bette Davis and Marlene Dietrich were among the glamorous film stars who toyed enticingly with cigarettes, while Groucho Marx and Orson Welles emphasized their masculinity by remaining true to the cigar. Winston Churchill was also devoted to the cigar; other British prime ministers, including Stanley Baldwin and Harold Wilson, were wedded to their pipes.

The 1950s saw two major developments. The first was the use of television to promote cigarettes, for example the phenomenally popular show *I Love Lucy*, sponsored by Philip Morris, began in 1951. The 1960s saw massive TV promotions. These included the memorable but ineffective 'You're never alone with a Strand', and the highly successful Marlboro Man and Marlboro Country. Another medium was the sponsorship of Formula One racing cars by tobacco companies. The second development was the introduction of filter tips and an emphasis on mildness and low levels of nicotine and tar, as tobacco companies reacted to increasing concerns about the harmful effects of cigarettes.

In 1964 a report from the US Surgeon General, Luther Terry, officially linked smoking and cancer and led to the imposition of health warnings on cigarette packs in the following year. In 1970 the US Congress required the warnings to be made more explicit and also banned cigarette advertising on radio and TV. A further report from the Surgeon General in 1988 concluded that nicotine was an addictive drug. The 1990s saw bans on smoking on airlines and interstate buses. In 2003 New York City banned smoking in all public places.

Similar moves took place in other countries. In the UK, for example, cigarette advertising was banned on TV from 1965 and on radio from 1971. Tobacco companies resorted to more subtle ways of selling their wares and in 1983 Saatchi and Saatchi launched the highly successful product-free advertisement for Silk Cut. Not until 2003 were newspapers banned from carrying tobacco advertising. Concerns about safety now matched those of health. In 1987 a fire at King's Cross underground station which led to the deaths of 31 people was attributed to a dropped cigarette or match and led to a complete ban on smoking in any part of London's underground system. Non-smokers were also shown to be at risk from 'passive smoking', and in 2002 the British Medical Association reported that there was no safe level of environmental tobacco smoke. Warnings on cigarette packs, such as 'Smoking Damages Your Health' or 'Smoking Kills', now took on an extra dimension. Cigarette smoke drifting across a private space such as a home or a public one like a restaurant or pub might be a danger to anyone in its path. Bans on smoking in public places have been introduced in many countries since the late 1990s.

Lessons from history

There are three major lessons to be drawn from this brief excursion into the history of smoking.

The first is that for most of human history people have not smoked tobacco. Until five centuries ago, smoking was confined to the inhabitants of one continent.

The second lesson is that there can be no doubt that smoking is here to stay for the foreseeable future. Indeed, smoking is still on the increase in those countries where governments are unenlightened and smokers uninformed. For example, recent surveys in China and India suggest that most smokers there are unaware of the harmful effects of tobacco. Even where restrictions are in place, tobacco is widely smuggled.

The third and by far the most important lesson is that Corti was wrong when he concluded that no government could ever reverse and restrict the spread of smoking. The historic turning point came in 1950 when evidence about the harmful effects of smoking became clear. In that year the British epidemiologist Richard Doll and a colleague published the results of a study which showed that among 649 lung-cancer cases there were only two non-smokers. Doll was so stunned by the findings that heavy smokers were 50 times more likely to contract lung cancer than non-smokers that he gave up smoking himself. Similar studies published in 1950 in the *Journal of the American Medical Association* reached the same conclusion – that heavy smokers were at a vastly increased risk of lung cancer. Four years later the results from Doll's further study of 40,000 doctors were so convincing that the British health minister, Iain Macleod, called a press conference at which, while chain-smoking himself, he was compelled to announce that 'It must be regarded as established that there is a relationship between smoking and cancer of the lung'.

Examples of prominent heavy smokers who died of lung cancer include the screen hero Humphrey Bogart in 1957 and the journalist and TV presenter Edward Murrow in 1965. But the most telling victim was Marlboro Man himself, Wayne McLaren. By 1972 the clean-living, clean-air image of the cowboy Marlboro Man had made Marlboro the world's bestselling cigarette. In 1992, however, a sickened McLaren appeared at the annual meeting of the shareholders of Philip Morris in Richmond, Virginia, and asked the company at least to limit its advertising. The chairman, Michael Morris, gave this chilling response: 'We're certainly sorry to hear about your medical problem. Without knowing your medical history, I don't want to comment any further.' Two years later Marlboro Man died of lung cancer. He was 51 years old.

Smoking kills. In the second half of the 20th century, as people became aware of its harmful effects, the tide of smoking was reversed. For example, in 1949, 81 per cent of men in the UK smoked. By 1972 the percentage had fallen below 50 per cent. Ten years later it was less than 40 per cent. A similar trend occurred in the USA where between 1965 and 1990 the percentage of adults who smoked declined from 42 per cent to 25 per cent. A study from 1997 revealed that 48 million US smokers had given up in the previous 21 years, while of the 48 million who continued to smoke, 34 million said that they wanted to quit.

With the aid of this book everyone who wants to stop smoking can.

Solution 19

History shows that scientific evidence about the harmful effects of smoking has led to a dramatic decline in the numbers of smokers in several countries, including the UK and USA.

20

Better sex

However good you feel you are at sex and however much you think you enjoy it, as a smoker you are missing out simply because your blood does not flow as well as that of someone who is a non-smoker. For both young and old sexually active people, this has got to be a big deterrent. And it gets worse. If you are thinking of starting a family, you must realize that you are not only damaging your health, but also, whatever your age, you are damaging your sperm and the chances of fertilization. This is not an attempt to scare you into stopping smoking but an obvious truth. If you are a healthy male or female and you are looking for a partner to fall in love with and raise a family, how would you choose? Would you opt for the person who sits on the sofa each night finishing off their pack of 20 Superkings, or for the partner who can walk you up a hill into the woods and demonstrate their athletic ability? In the movies, lovers are often depicted as having a smoke immediately after having sex. Could the reason for having a smoke after sex be because these people are tired out and cannot summon the energy to do it again, while the non-smokers are still at it?

It could be that the smokers, after all their hard work, are craving a cigarette but if that is so, please answer this next question. How many times during sex do you think of:

▶ Margaret Thatcher

▶ Ozzy Osbourne

▶ smoking.

Unless you are Sharon Osbourne or the late Sir Denis Thatcher, I would hope that none of those images has ever flashed into your mind; but there is probably more chance of those two faces popping into your head than the need for a smoke. When was the last time you were having sex and you said halfway through foreplay, 'Hang on, darling, it's time for a smoke break'? The reason you reach for or crave a smoke is that you associate smoking with relaxing and you are generally very relaxed when you have just finished making love to your partner. The problem is that if you smoke and your partner does not, there is nothing more of a turn-off than kissing somebody who has choked down a few gallons of smoke. Or imagine lying there

after sex and all you're thinking of is that you fancy a cigarette, while the non-smoker is lying there thinking, 'I hope we can do that again very soon.'

When your mind is occupied, it is much easier to go without a cigarette, but as soon as your mind has a rest or has no specific focus, it reminds itself to top up on nicotine before you start to get those slight withdrawal symptoms. I am not saying that you should spend your whole life having sex, but this example does highlight how smoking can interrupt your life as well as detract from it. Which brings us to another point. Smoking does not improve your concentration. Quite the opposite! It is more likely to break your concentration.

There are many times in life when you are so occupied with work or pleasure, including when having sex, that you do not notice any craving for a cigarette. For example, if you were watching a good movie at the cinema it would seem stupid to go out and have a smoke. When you are watching a bad movie it seems quite reasonable to go out once or twice to relieve your cravings. It almost sounds like a good way of finding out how much an audience likes a film. Take 200 smokers into a cinema to watch a film and measure how good or bad the film is by how many cigarettes they smoke out the back. It could even be a standardized test – the cough test. The more the audience smokes, the more they cough, and the less they like the film.

To return to the point! Even though I have researched this aspect of sex and our reproductive health in depth, I did not have to look far for information about whether smoking has a detrimental effect on your reproductive organs. Written on the side and front of many cigarette packs are statements such as 'Smoking damages your sperm' and 'Smoking harms your unborn baby'.

Smoking babies

My most vivid memory of an expectant mother smoking was when I was 16 years old, at Surbiton train station, south of London. A friend and I had just missed the connecting train home after a party. It was too late to ring anyone for a lift home so we were sitting on the steps outside the station having a smoke before the ten-mile walk back to my house. As we sat there, a couple of young women came over to join us and ask for some cigarettes. They were both in their mid-twenties and had also been out partying that evening and they were waiting for a taxi home. We did not have enough money for a taxi but we did have enough for a pack of cigarettes from the all-night petrol station three miles down the road.

As I looked at one of the women lighting up I could not miss the enormous bump sticking out of her elasticated trousers.

She noticed me staring and told me that she was trying to cut down. 'Weren't we all?' As they both sat down to join us the pregnant woman explained that this was her second child and this pregnancy was a lot less hassle than the first one. You might wonder why I remember this little story so well. It was not because she was a pregnant mother smoking but because of what happened next. The friend who was with the pregnant woman joked that the reason this baby was more subdued was because she smoked and drank more. As I forced out a smile, the pregnant woman pulled out a four-pack of Special Brew from her bag and offered us one to share. We sat with these women telling bad jokes, smoking and drinking very strong lager until their taxi came, and got a lift as far as the petrol station so it saved us a bit of our walk. As a teenager I related that story to many of my friends at school and they all said how bad it was that she was drinking extra-strong beer. Not one of them seemed bothered by the smoking!

That was 28 years ago, when there was not the degree of awareness and the information that there is today about the damaging effects of smoke on an unborn or newly born baby. Thankfully, there is much greater support from the government and National Health Service in relation to smoking and pregnant mothers. In England the health service is using mobile phones to help motivate mothers to cut out smoking. They take pictures from the scan of the developing baby in the womb and put them as screen savers on the mother's phone. Every time the mother feels the urge to light up, she looks at the picture of her unborn baby to inspire her not to smoke.

When I was a smoker, many of the pregnant women that I sat with on the fire escape at work smoked. Every one of them told me that they were only smoking a few but they needed to have a few to get through their day. At social events I have seen women telling off expectant mothers who smoke for not caring about their unborn children and I have seen many more people scowling from a distance. I recognize that being pregnant definitely seems to have its highs and lows. For some women it can be a stressful situation and a time of nervousness as they feel their body is being taken over by somebody else.

Other women seem to be naturals at it and walk around with a beautiful glow.

If you are a woman planning to have children or already pregnant and you still smoke, you probably don't need me to make you feel more guilty than you already do. Many of us already know about the harmful effects smoking has on babies while their fragile bodies develop inside their mothers. What goes into your body goes into your baby's body, but at least you have an immune system and strong, developed lungs. After the baby is born your smoking addiction can have a big influence on its health and behaviour, even if you do not smoke anywhere near them. If you breastfeed, then you pass nicotine through your milk, turning your little one into an innocent nicotine junkie who can only get a fix from its mother's breast.

In one way smoking mothers almost confirm that they need to smoke because none of them would choose to smoke while pregnant. I have heard many people wish that they could stop, but none more than would-be mothers. It is not your fault that you started smoking, but it *is* your fault if you carry on after reading this book, because now you know how to avoid the trap and you no longer want to be tricked at the expense of your health, sanity and unborn child. Smoking is not the necessity that you once thought it was, and it has never been the pleasure that our brains made it out to be. You stop smoking by breaking the chain of events that keep you an addict and that is as simple as not having the next cigarette.

Solution 20
Better sex; healthier babies.

21

Buy your own cigarettes

So you have got yourself down to just five cigarettes a day. You can nab a smoke from your colleague whom you sit next to when you get to work. And then there is John and Suneeta who always go for a cigarette at coffee time by the fire escape who don't seem to mind donating to a semi-retired smoker. At lunchtime there are all the delivery guys outside who are always friendly and generous and you can normally last until the walk to the station with Debs, the receptionist, who smokes like a chimney and catches the same train home as you. At home you have a small pack of ten cigarettes that you can dip into for the extra one or two. If you have a long phone call to make or friends come round for a drink then there is the petrol station round the corner for a fresh pack.

In your mind you have cracked it; in everyone else's mind you resemble a crack addict, but you seem not to have noticed. You have this clever idea that each month you will cut out one cigarette each day and in five months you will have stopped. In fact, you think this idea is so clever you are going to write a book called *The Five-Month Plan* or is it *The Five- (Maybe Eight-) Month Plan* and retire to Cuba on the royalties.

After a few weeks, people are getting a bit irritated and tell you that you should buy your own cigarettes. Even your loyal train companion Debs has had enough; she has bought you a fresh pack, left them on your desk and asked you for a fiver to cover the cost. You have had enough of this and you go out and buy two of the most popular brands of cigarettes and make a point of being very generous with your cigarettes so that you can build up credits for your next failed attempt at quitting smoking. While sitting out by the fire escape you discover that all the smokers have been talking behind your back and have actually had a wager going on how long it will be before you started bringing in your own pack. This to you seems normal and you sit back and enjoy the fact that you are at one and back with your fellow smokers.

Unfortunately, until the point that your brain works out that smoking is the actual cause of the whole problem and not the solution, these and similar situations and pretend remedies only serve to confirm that you enjoy smoking and you need

LEAD ME NOT INTO TEMPTATION

to smoke. The other problem is that when you are asking for advice on how to deal with trying to stop smoking you are always asking the wrong people – smokers! They do not want you to stop. If you, one of the least successful people at stopping smoking, ever actually managed to stop, it would mean that anyone could do it. They have been watching you try and fail for ages. Your failure confirms to everyone else that you are happier as a smoker and so are they.

This is obviously rubbish! When you do stop smoking (which will be soon) it will confirm one thing. That is: you never wanted to do it in the first place, and once you understand the messages about smoking contained in this book you will also understand that teaching yourself to stop smoking is an easy thing to do. Your smoker friends do not want you to stop because it will take away one of their reasons for lighting up. It will take away their precious excuses for sucking down more smoke and there will be one less companion on the fire escape.

Solution 21

Any attempt to limit or control your nicotine intake highlights the fact that you are never in control of smoking. If you carry on smoking, it carries on dictating your life.

22

Young smokers

Boys and girls, young men and women of the future who are not yet voters (age 18 in the UK) have more right to be angry than any other age group. Since the 1960s, many retail companies and other businesses have realized the importance of targeting you in their sales campaigns. One reason for this is that you spend a higher proportion of your money on yourselves than adults. A second reason is that if companies can attract young people like you to buy their products at an early age, you are more likely to continue with those brands in the future. And I do mean boys and girls, young men and women. Recent research shows that 19 per cent of 15-year-old girls in England are regular smokers.

Another major factor in targeting younger people is that you are a very controllable group of consumers. Advertisers use a variety of media – television, magazines, films, music and sport are just some examples – to project enticing images associated with their products. These include the clothes you wear, from trainers to T-shirts, the music you listen to, mobile phones and computer games and other modern gadgetry. Yet the driving force behind all this advertising is simply to make as much money as possible for the companies that produce, distribute and sell the goods.

Most of these products will not do you any harm, but one certainly will. Tobacco companies do not care whether you live or die; their object is to make a profit. Some people associated with these companies really do not care; others perhaps do not understand the full consequences of what they do.

At the end of the day you have some choice about how to spend your money. If you feel like wearing the same football boots as your favourite football hero, or wearing the same style clothes as your favourite band or singer, that's cool. My big influences when I was 13 years old were hip-hop and breakdancing, skateboarding, BMX racing and athletics. By the age of 15 I was friends with some top graffiti artists, was competing in a breakdance crew and had been offered sponsorship in freestyle BMX. I am sure that would not be everyone's ideal choice of what they wanted to do with part of their teenage life, but those influences from my younger years have carried through into middle age. I can still be found practising on a half pipe with my skateboard (when no one's looking), I still feel the need to get down when I hear some funky hip-hop, and surfing is a very big part of my life.

When I was young, all the older kids around me smoked and it seemed natural to make it a permanent part of my life without any real thought. I can remember from the age of 11 making fun of the kids who used to choke every time they tried to take down a lungful of smoke. It was as if they were not grown-up enough to cope with it, unlike my friends and me. Looking back, I would have been a lot better off if I had choked and coughed every time I sucked on a cigarette; at least then I might not have carried on smoking. As a young smoker or someone who is thinking of taking up smoking, I cannot tell exactly how you view smoking – you have to answer that for yourself. But when my mates and I were younger we thought it was cool, adult and adventurous, and smoking made us feel sort of independent. What rubbish that turned out to be!

If you are a pre-teen or teenager reading this, you are probably a lot smarter than I was as a kid, and you already suspect or know that smoking is something you would prefer not to have in your life. If you have been smoking for a while, the problem is that your brain may already have been fooled into thinking you enjoy smoking. If you are already at the stage of blowing smoke-rings and own a nice-looking Zippo or a fancy lighter, you can take that as a definite yes. Even if you are at the stage where you are mainly smoking handouts and then buying a pack of ten twice a week, you are already addicted! Don't worry; it is easy to stop once you have got your head around the idea. Smoking is an addictive con that tobacco companies use to rip you off. It has no benefit to you and can affect your well-being and performance even though you are young and healthy.

Through advertising and clever marketing, tobacco companies can influence you into taking up smoking, but the natural mixing of young kids with teenage smokers is where most of us first come across cigarettes. One of the ways that the tobacco companies make it easier for young people to take up smoking is with the size of a pack of cigarettes. Why do you think that they still sell packs of ten cigarettes in the UK? It is because cigarettes are expensive for younger people (especially in the UK) and selling them in cheaper, smaller packs makes them easier for you to get hold of. In the USA, cigarettes are a lot cheaper so they are only sold in packs of 20. I remember the first time I ordered a pack of cigarettes in the USA, I asked for a pack of 20 Marlboro Lights and the lady gave me 400 cigarettes. I had been so used to asking for either a pack of 20 or a pack of ten in the UK that I always asked for my smokes with the description of what size pack I wanted. I did try to persuade the lady behind the counter that I only wanted one pack and not 20, but she explained to me that it was a whole lot cheaper if I bought in bulk. Back then it worked out at around 50p a pack so it was not hard to afford them; we agreed on only ten packs of 20 and I would come back next week for the other 200.

Smoking has become much more expensive than in the past, but once you are hooked on smoking you will always find a way of getting cigarettes. Even if I told you that you are better off throwing the money away than spending it on cigarettes, you would think that a waste and me an idiot for saying it. If you already smoke, think back to the time when you did not. Did you ever have an urge to run off somewhere and set fire to a big, fat piece of weed and suck on it? The problem is that once you are addicted to smoking you have to do it. You may not really have thought about it, but at certain times of the day you have this urge to light up. If you are at school or at home with disapproving parents, you obviously have to be a little subtle about how you do it, but nevertheless, even though sometimes you wish that you did not smoke, you still have to do it. Unfortunately you are not making the choice to smoke; the nicotine in your brain, delivered into your bloodstream by the cigarette you just smoked, is making that choice for you. The more you understand why you smoke, the easier it is not to do it. The sooner you realize that you are being lied to by large corporations and fooled by a cunning chemical trick, the sooner you can give smoking a miss.

As teenagers, when we are warned by adults not to drink alcohol, smoke and have sex, our first reaction may be that these adults just do not understand what it is like to be young today. They do. It was no different in their day. Their concern is genuine and their experience is valuable. Whatever age we are, young or old, we can all benefit from the advice of those who are more experienced than ourselves, and especially from adults who have our real best interests at heart. The tobacco companies do not have your best interests at heart; they are interested in their profits. If you look through some of the marketing strategies and paperwork of the large tobacco companies, you will find that they have phrases such as 'a cigarette for the beginner is a symbolic act. It means I am no longer my mother's child, I'm tough, I am an adventurer . . .'. The tobacco companies know their young target audience all too well. They understand that you want to move on and to be, and appear to be, more mature. That is chemically built into us all when we are growing up. Many young people see their first drink or first sexual experience as a part of moving into adulthood. At the right time and in moderation these can be pleasant and proper experiences.

But smoking is not a part of adulthood – completely the reverse. Tobacco companies know that the best time to get people hooked on smoking is before they are 16. Between the ages of 11 and 16 you are very susceptible to peer pressure and following the latest trends. As many of you know already, by the time you realize that you do not want to smoke you already feel that you cannot stop. I remember at college when I was only 16 or 17 trying to stop many times. I used to try to just smoke a third of a cigarette between classes and kept the stinking butts in a tin, but it made smoking seem even more desirable. If I had known then what I know now, I could have stopped in one minute and never wanted to smoke again. Luckily, I know now!

When you see other people smoking, how do you think they look? Does smoking seem sophisticated, clever, adult, enjoyable, exciting? At school we used to go to the other side of the park for our lunchtime smoke. If it was only a short break, we had to chance it round by the side entrance to the school. It was difficult to squeeze a smoke in at this time of day, but the problem was that if I did not manage a quick one, I would be irritable and unable to concentrate until lunchtime. But as this book makes clear, smoking does not help you to concentrate. It just relieves the annoying, nagging feeling that it created in the first place. A smoker's life is punctuated by withdrawal symptoms. Not smoking gets rid of those withdrawal symptoms forever. Because I used to hang out and play basketball in the gym during the lunch break, sometimes I would not have enough time to get across the park. So if no one was around, I would have to chance a quick smoke in the toilets and risk turning up late for class. It must have been very obvious to the teachers what kids had been doing when they turned up a little late with some poxy excuse and stinking of cigarettes. These days, teachers have a lot more to worry about than another kid smoking. They have seen it a thousand times before and unfortunately will see it many times again.

For those of you who are really into sport, there is no way you can afford to smoke. You might get away with it while you are still at the handout stage of smoking, but once you are at the addicted level of buying your own there will be a definite decline in your lung capacity and fitness. I was always fighting to keep my smoking under control because I was into a lot of sport. When I hit 16 and went to college and had a part-time job, I started smoking more and the level at which I played sport took a definite decline. I certainly regretted the way I coughed after a cross-country race or the blueness in my face from hyperventilating after running a few lengths of a basketball court. How many athletes do you see lighting up after they have just won a race or match?

When you look at non-smokers, do they seem to be missing out on something? If you are a smoker, do you think that you have found something that is enjoyable and that some of your friends

are missing out because they do not smoke? What an absolute pile of pants! Ask any person over the age of 20 if they want to stop smoking or whether they would recommend smoking to you. No one is going to recommend smoking to you. Even people you know that have smoked for many years are only doing so because they think it is too difficult to give up. That is not the case; the sooner you stop the better, and the sooner you stop the easier it is. The reason the people around you still smoke is that as yet they have not been given or processed the information that you have acquired from reading some of this book. Once they have done so, they will understand that there is no point in carrying on smoking.

You should remember that young smokers are ripped off and conned by an industry that knows it can take advantage of them because they are less knowledgeable about its tricks and traps. If I put the same chemicals that are in cigarettes in dog turds and fed them to you for a month, you would end up thinking you liked dog turds. That's right. Instead of popping behind the bike sheds for a smoke, you would be gagging for a nicotine-filled pile of poo. How cool would that be? You would soon become even less attractive to the opposite sex than with the stink of cigarettes you already have.

Luckily for you, smoking is on the decline in much of the developed world. And hopefully the same will soon apply in other developed and developing countries. In many parts of the world, including states on the European, American and Australasian continents, governments have introduced laws to control or even ban advertising of tobacco products. One way of seeing how attitudes have changed is to look at the percentage of people smoking in the films of the mid-20th century. Virtually all the characters seemed to smoke, whatever they were doing or about to do – from driving a car to killing a bad guy, finishing a dance routine or even kissing the leading lady.

Until recently you could still buy cigarette sweets in the UK. These were either sugar candy in the design of a cigarette with a red end, or chocolate rollups that were chocolate shaped as smokes and rolled in edible rice paper. They would come in boxes that looked just like a pack of cigarettes. As kids we would pretend to smoke these sweets before we ate them. We were just copying a lot of other people of the time, whether it was people in the street or movie stars in films; we were pretending to be grown up. In many countries around the world you can still find sweet cigarettes that use slight variations of well-known brand names. Instead of Marlboro you have Marlbaro; Pall Mali instead of Pall Mall; Enson & Hedge instead of Benson & Hedges, and my favourite, Acmel in place of Camel.

An interesting survey in the late 1980s showed that tobacco advertising was reaching the very young. Camel was one brand I used to smoke. The promotion logo was a cool, sunglasses-wearing, big, smiling camel called Joe Camel. He was drawn as a cartoon character, and cards with this camel character in some funny pose came with every pack. To my mind, the image that Camel cigarettes tried to portray was that of a slightly adventurous, cool but tough, go-anywhere kind of smoke, a lot like the Marlboro brand. I even had a Camel lighter and a pair of camel sunglasses. A medical journal reported on a survey of a large group of children aged three to six years old, where the children were shown a picture of Joe Camel and asked what they associated with the picture. Some 96 per cent of these children said that they connected that image with smoking. For some of the age group Joe Camel was more recognizable than Mickey Mouse. Even though in many countries smoking and its advertising power are on the decline, if you are reading this book or have been given this chapter to read, then you or someone else has rightly decided that it is not declining quickly enough.

Remember that most smokers start when they are young, before they are fully grown and aware of or even care about the pitfalls of smoking and the con that it is. If you are a young smoker, by the time you start to understand the real rip-off that smoking is, your brain is telling you that you need to smoke. The two most likely reactions to advice to stop smoking are either to switch off or to believe that the person telling you to stop does not understand the pleasure that you get from smoking. Chances are, the person who is telling you not to smoke cares about you and does not want to see you wasting part of your life through smoking. Remember, if you really like smoking, why can't you just do it once every couple of weeks? Why do you have this urge to do it whenever you can? If smoking is so great, why is almost every adult smoker you know talking about how they are going to give up or how they wish they had never started? The sooner you stop the better you feel! The sooner you see smoking for what it really is – the biggest con of the modern world, especially aimed at the under-twenties – the better for you. Then it becomes easy to see why you thought that you liked doing it, even though actually you didn't enjoy it at first. Once free yourself, when you see people smoking you will not envy them but instead end up pitying them. And at the same time you will understand how great it is that you do not have to smoke ever again.

Many of the kids from local schools who smoke use the cul-de-sac where I live as their smoking alley as they know that not many people are going to be there, and it is unlikely that any of the teachers would look for them there or pass that way. I have used their comments, and those of many other young people who smoke, to understand better their views and reasons for smoking. Understandably, when asked why they smoke, most of them do not reply that they are nicotine junkies fooled by tobacco companies into being slaves and dragged down by their black lungs towards financial ruin and an early death only to profit a few tobacco company employees. Many say they like it; some that they feel that is a sociable thing; others that it is something to do instead of being bored. My aim with this chapter is to show you that these reasons are not enough. If this chapter has given you some understanding of why you really smoke – to get a nicotine fix – please let me encourage you to read the whole book. That way you really will be convinced that your life in future will be much better without a cigarette hanging out of your mouth and smoke blowing out of your nose. Ask adults who smoke whether they wish they had never started smoking. When you hear their replies, ask yourself why they all say 'YES'.

Rolling a fat one

By the time I was 14 many of the social events catering for my own age group and older kids involved some amount of drugs. I hope that these paragraphs do not relate to you, but things have not changed much over the years. If you already smoke, it is definitely easier to smoke something that is passed to you by a friend or at a party. If you have had some experience of smoking drugs, then at some point you are going to have to decide whether those substances improve your life or hold you back from doing the things you really want to do. Luckily most of the softer drugs that you can smoke do not have the immediate addictive nature of nicotine. But that is not to say they are less harmful or do not take their toll on you in some other way.

Some of my friends used to start their day with a joint and a cup of coffee. The ones that still do that either seem to have lost the plot in their lives or have weak immune systems. Many people who get into smoking drugs are also likely to experiment with stronger drugs and that is when you run into problems really fast, especially if you are young and your mind is still developing. I have friends who have been institutionalized because their brains could not tell up from down, purely from taking too much of the wrong drugs.

Many people reading this book could say that smoking a few too many spliffs has a less harmful effect than drinking too much alcohol. At least if you smoke too much grass or skunk, you do not get moody and want to be violent; you probably just fall asleep. My hope for all of you is that you reach part, if not all, of your potential, so that you can enjoy your short time on this earth and benefit yourselves and others with your abilities, whatever they are. It would be great for everyone to be happy, healthy and drug-free, but as we all know, through our own or other people's experience, that is not always the case. Some of us have to get knocked down a few times before we realize how to stand on our own two feet. Sometimes the people who get knocked back the hardest are the ones who achieve their dreams. Unfortunately, that does not happen often!

This book does not contain information on drugs other than nicotine, even though there are similarities. So if smoking drugs is a part of your life, you should urgently seek other help. Otherwise you will miss the life you are supposed to be living because your mind is somewhere else.

Solution 22

Whatever age you are, now is the time to say that you are fed up with being conned by the tobacco companies and their clever chemical trick.

23

Will I put on weight?

I suppose the answer you want to hear at this point is a resounding 'No!'. Well, read on and make your own decision.

There is an idea that smoking, just like food, provides the emotional comfort we need when we feel dissatisfied or unloved; that a cigarette could be considered as an emotional dummy or our old favourite blanket or soft toy. Alternatively, there is the explanation of never having been breastfed and a lack of proper nurture from our mothers. Do we try to compensate by continually putting something in our mouths? This may be a lovely, sweet-sounding excuse, that back in your childhood you were not cuddled enough and because of that you took up smoking and it is not your fault. Not true! Unfortunately, you were targeted by an unscrupulous dealer who made you into a nicotine addict. You smoke because you are a NICOTINE JUNKIE who needs a fix. You smoke because you are addicted to a drug that, if you do not have it, makes you feel uneasy. And because your brain has not worked out the subtle effects of this drug, it can turn you into a right pain in the posterior if you don't have it.

Hunger is an everyday feeling that we understand. If we feel empty inside, we find ourselves some food and that makes us feel comfortable. Take away food and hunger soon starts to affect our emotions and ability to function properly. If without food for a while, most of us become irritable and unable to concentrate, or we can get moody if we do not have our natural sugar fix at some point during the day. Go without eating for a day or two and we lack the will and strength to carry out the simplest of tasks, as we feel too weak and tired.

The slightly empty, irritating sensation of craving nicotine that you experience when you stop smoking is similar to that sensation of feeling hungry. But when you feel that sensation, no amount of food will take its place. Even if you eat the entire contents of a sweet shop, you will not find the exact flavour you are looking for; you will still feel that you must find just one more flavour. All you need to do is realize that the craving for nicotine is being mistaken for hunger and this sensation will soon pass.

When I stopped smoking I actually lost weight. My food definitely tasted better and I stopped suffering from indigestion.

I found that because I knew what the empty craving for nicotine really needed to satisfy it, I did not try to replace smoking with food. What I replaced it with was answers, which meant that I snacked less as a non-smoker than as a smoker. It is interesting to know that in Chinese medicine, smoking is described as causing heat in the lungs and stomach. The presence of heat in an organ tends to upset its function and exacerbate any underlying weakness. Perhaps I was always bolting my food down so I could rush outside and have a smoke, and that was causing my indigestion. You obviously have the choice to eat more or to eat less. Whether you are one of those people who is always struggling with their weight or you can easily choose a bowl of fruit salad over a pack of chocolate Hobnobs, I would say this to you:

- you are going to feel much better about yourself because of not smoking

- you will feel much more in control of your life because of not wanting to smoke

- you are going to have more energy than before and become more active

- you are going to enjoy every mouthful of food much more as your taste buds improve

- you will not care if you put on a few pounds, because you are going to feel so good about yourself

- you have the control to do anything you want

- you are the one who makes the choices and decisions.

Statistics show that smokers are less active than non-smokers. This is particularly the case among older people. Either smokers have less energy to get up and go, or active people do not want to smoke.

All people who stop smoking find that their overall health benefits. You will feel the need to be more active as you will have more energy and more time in your day to get things done. I am not saying that you are going to join the nearest gym and should rummage around for that old leotard. I am saying that you will feel better about yourself and your body and will want to get more use out it. Think about it; for many years you have been telling your body not to worry about poisoning itself and making stupid excuses every time that you do it. That's a bit like telling yourself, 'This is not going to hurt' just before you purposely stub your toe again and again. Even if you do not think it with every cigarette you smoke, that thought is somewhere in your head every time you light up. Once you have stopped smoking, your brain and your body are going to get along and feel a lot better.

Weighty issues

If you are a person who has an issue with food, you must realize that this is a separate issue even though there are similarities with smoking. If, when you are feeling down, you always reach for chocolate or cakes, along with a milkshake and a couple of Danish pastries, you probably understand that there is a problem. One problem is that you may feel guilty and uncomfortable. How do you deal with that problem? By putting something else in your mouth? If you are too full and uncomfortable to eat any more, then the temptation is to smoke, as a cigarette is the only thing that will fit. This compounds the situation and leaves you feeling unhappy with yourself and in need of more comfort. Once you can see smoking for what it is, you can stop. Once you realize that many of those high-fat and sugary foods don't make you feel better but worse, you can start to help yourself to a healthier life. Your ingrained reaction from an early age is to see rich food as a treat and a pleasure. The quick rush that you get from those sugary foods gives you a quick fix but soon after leaves you with less energy and feelings of lethargy, so it is no wonder that you are tempted to get another sugar fix. When you were younger you were more energetic, and you probably did not eat entire packs of chocolate or biscuits in one go. Just as when you were younger you were not free to smoke as much as you wanted.

Once you understand that you never wanted to smoke and that you unfortunately fell into its trap at an earlier age, you can stop smoking. Once you have stopped smoking you can start to deal with any overindulgence with food. When you can see smoking for what it is, it will become easier to tell what makes your body feel bad or good. Heavy fats and sugars in food do have a slightly addictive nature, but not to the same extent as nicotine. Unfortunately, to explain that fully would take up half the book. The type of foodstuffs that you put in your body determine your weight and the way you feel. If you believe that you have a problem with your weight or sugar intake, you need to look at foods and think how they make you feel after you have eaten them. For example, if I look at a big cream cake, I know that it does not taste as good as feeling fit and healthy does. Which means that even though the initial taste seems satisfying, what it does to you and how it makes you feel afterwards is ten times less pleasurable.

Obviously we need to eat, but we do not need to smoke. You need to eat and you need to feel good about yourself to carry on with your life. Being out of control in life can sometimes be fun, but being out of control of your body is not. You can be any weight that you want to be as long as it makes you feel happy, but if it does not, you need to address that situation sooner rather than later. You are reading this book to stop smoking because you have decided you no longer want to smoke and you need some help and encouragement. Even though there are positive points about not smoking that relate to losing weight or eating a healthier diet, there is no point in being unnecessarily hard on yourself. Once you realize that eating more does not satisfy the craving for nicotine, you can deal with those early cravings to smoke. Once you have dealt with those and confirmed that you never want to put nicotine in your system again, you can start to look at what you eat and what makes you feel good.

Even if you are one of those people who tends to rush straight for the chocolates when you are feeling low or under pressure, you must be starting to realize that you are going to feel great when you stop smoking. You are about to take back control of a part of your life that has held you back for many years. So even if you put on a few pounds at first as you reach for another biscuit (and it certainly doesn't have to be that way), you can sit back and smile and tell yourself how wonderful it is that you do not have to smoke any more.

A healthy balance

There is nothing wrong with being an emotional person; for many it can greatly add to the adventure we call life. Smoking, along with other substances that we put into our bodies, chemically controls your mood and that is a fact. **So why wait for the right feeling to kick in when you already know the action that will make you feel better?**

Having an understanding of how your blood sugars can affect your mood, energy levels and feelings of stress can greatly help you to understand and deal with your body's cravings. Our bodies are designed to cope with a certain amount of stress and the way they deal with it is always the same, whether the stress is created through joy, upset, hunger, thirst, fear, injury, fatigue or overstimulation. When our blood sugar levels are too high or too low, our body thinks we are in a state of stress and acts to deal with it. If we have let our sugar levels get too low, our brain starts to shut down non-essential functions to keep us going. It tells us when we are tired, stressed, thirsty or need to eat. If we choose not to take that advice, it activates our adrenal glands; insulin levels fall, cortisol levels rise and more glucose is released from the liver into the blood, preparing us to deal with the stressful situation we are in. In prehistoric times, when we ran away from scary things or chased down our food before we could eat it, a short burst of adrenaline to boost our energy levels was most useful. In addition, by being very physically active we burnt off the chemicals in our body created by the stressful situation. Even if our blood sugar levels are in a balanced state, overstimulating the body with substances like nicotine puts the body into a state of stress, causing a spike in our sugar levels. If our sugar levels go up, they must come down and unless we address our bodies' need to balance them, we struggle and become exhausted or rely on stimulants to keep us going. This causes more strain and stress on the body in the long term.

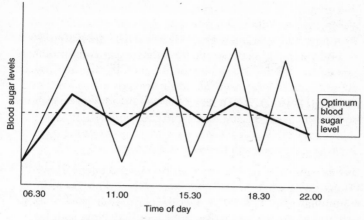

Blood sugar levels — Time of day: 06.30, 11.00, 15.30, 18.30, 22.00

Optimum blood sugar level

——— The ideal range within which blood sugar levels should rise and fall throughout the day.

——— The extreme highs and lows of blood sugar levels if the body is running on fast-burning sugars and stimulants.

- - - - The optimum blood sugar level.

Remember this

If your blood sugar levels rise and fall rapidly throughout the day, you are in a higher state of stress and more likely to crave a stimulant like nicotine.

Imagine this. You start your day, as you would expect, with low blood sugars. Two strong, sweet coffees and a few cigarettes later, for a short time you feel your body has had a kick-start and you're raring to go. You have already caused a spike in your blood sugar levels and the crash is coming shortly but you fend it off with a sugary fruit juice and a bagel and you feel good to go again. You manage to survive on the stimulating kick of one more coffee and some smokes to get you through to lunchtime. By lunchtime you are starving. You do your best to choose a healthy option but you go heavy on the sweet potato fries, which overload your body in the short term so your blood sugar levels drop. Even though you cannot be hungry, you crave something sweet to keep you awake at work. By the time you are back at your desk you are finding it difficult not to fall asleep, and even though it's an easy day you feel under stress. By 4 p.m. and after a few more cigarettes you are getting your second wind, and because you are meeting a friend for dinner, you decide not to eat anything until 8 p.m. By the time you get to the restaurant, your blood sugar levels are so low you could eat a waiter. When they offer you bread, you take enough to feed the five thousand and while your body is trying to digest your biblical snack you over-order for your main course because your body still thinks it is starving.

Let us pause a second before your two-pound burger arrives. Think about what the stress on your body is doing to your emotional state. You are all over the place; your sense of calm stopped soon after you woke in the morning. Now your body is digesting the bread you've eaten, so by the time your main course arrives you are not particularly hungry any more. But you have ordered the food, so you eat as much as you can, loosen the button on your trousers and try to be polite by just about staying awake to listen to your friend's recent adventure. Two strong coffees and three cigarettes later, you arrive home to find your partner has put the kids to bed, chilled a bottle of wine and has a big smile on their face. It might as well be a funnel and a colonic tube for the good it would do because you are feeling about as sexy as a neutered panda. But instead of being honest about how you feel and why, you bring up some pathetic argument from three days ago and end up alone in front of the TV, exhausted, chain-smoking and unable to go to sleep because you feel wired. You finally drift off to sleep but wake exhausted the next morning and the whole process starts again.

If you make some simple changes you can feel much better and have the energy you need to be alert at every moment of your day. By choosing foods and drinks that maintain constant blood sugar levels, you reduce the stress on your body and improve your performance. Managing your stress levels is key to controlling your cravings and maintaining a healthier body. The more balanced your body feels, the less the need for artificial stimulants and the easier it is to deal with your nicotine cravings. You have to work out what is realistic for you but you do need a plan. The feedback I get from people when they eat in a way that balances their blood sugars is: 'I never realized how bad I felt until I felt this good'. The better you eat, the less junk you crave. Look at food and decide how you want to feel. If you want to feel moody, tired, bloated and stressed, then eat junk food – but is it really what you want?

I am not going to give a long list of recipes and diet suggestions, as that would divert us from what you want to achieve, and you probably have a good idea of what makes you feel more balanced. If you have the choice between an apple and a small bowl of oatmeal with a fruit tea or two pastries and a hot chocolate, you can probably guess which option would cause a spike in your blood sugar levels and which one would maintain your energy levels for longer. What about pizza and garlic bread washed down with a large diet cola versus sweet potato, chicken, red onion and pepper kebabs washed down with a soda and fresh lime? Or for an evening meal, salmon stuffed with goats' cheese and sun-dried tomatoes in a mixed leaf salad versus spaghetti bolognaise with cheesy nachos? There are many books available on healthy eating and dieting; whatever you feel suits you, variety and moderation is the key. Having worked in the health and fitness industry for many years and tried most ways of eating at some point, I see great results in those people who follow something similar to the various paleo and caveman diet books. There are benefits for muscle tone, energy levels, positive mood, weight loss and general well-being. Interestingly, many of the people who write these books seem to combine a personal concern with health and a background in science that backs up their nutritional information. A few years ago I was diagnosed with a particular form of arthritis and I have also worked with hundreds of other people with arthritic conditions. I see a massive improvement in pain reduction and joint mobility among people who adopt a more paleo diet. I am not an expert in that field, so I can only comment on what I see, but you never know who might find that information helpful.

Many moderate to heavy smokers manage to get through to late lunchtime on diet drinks and coffee and then have one or two big meals later in the day. By the time they eat, their bodies are at such a low ebb that portions are often much bigger what their body needs and the meal is followed by a slump and a need for more stimulants. Tasty, delicious, small, satisfying meals and snacks throughout the day will give you all the energy and sense of balance to perform and function at your best. I see many people who stop smoking and lose weight and look better, partly because the control they now have over their body spills over into their eating habits. Not only do they look better, but they also have a sense of calmness as much of the anxiety and unwanted stress has left their body. When you are doing more of the things you want and have more energy, smoking seems like a waste of time.

Solution 23

Choose the foods that lift your mood.

24

I am having a bad day

Many readers of this book see cigarettes as loyal friends that will never let you down whatever is going on in your life. Some of the old tobacco advertising slogans used to say that you were never alone when you had that brand of cigarettes. Advertising is not the reason that you see a cigarette as your trusty pal; mental misconception is. Even before you started smoking, you perhaps had the idea that smoking was a useful tool in dealing with awkward situations or troubling times.

Your last request

If you were going in front of the firing squad and the man tying on your blindfold asked if there was anything you wanted, you would probably ask for a cigarette even if you did not smoke. It might be a better idea to ask for a very large, slow-burning cigar, to allow time for the cavalry to ride up and save your smoking behind. The other image that most of us have from films or books is that if you are shot and have to be left behind, your comrades always leave you with some smokes and a very large gun to take on the pursuing enemy. I have spoken to smokers who have been shot and they told me that they instinctively reached for a cigarette if they were able to. An old friend of mine, a former soldier, said that once the medic had tended to his wound, he pulled out a cigarette, lit it in his own mouth and then put it into my friend's mouth. The shot soldier took one big drag and then proceeded to choke. He told the medic that he would do better to shoot him than to give him another cigarette.

My own most uncomfortable need for smoking involved a motorcycle crash in the middle of the Welsh mountains. While blasting round the off-road tracks in the rocky terrain I took off on a jump and, showing off to a friend, I forgot the basic rule of landing wheels first and landed handlebars first. Even though we were in the middle of nowhere and I was unable to walk, my friend picked me up, put me on his bike and stuck it in second gear. Although I had a broken hand and leg, he guided me back over the five miles to the nearest road and then went to get help. While he was doing this, I was left with a few bent cigarettes and a dented can of Coke that blew up in my face when I opened it. Lying at the side of the road drinking my flat Coke and trying not to pass out, I thought it would be good to have a smoke to pass the time. Halfway through that cigarette the Coke exploded again, but this time it came out of me and all over the road. With the amount of adrenaline running around my system, the last thing my body needed was a nicotine hit to make the situation worse. Weirdly, half an hour later, when I really started to worry about whether my friend was coming back, I lit up another cigarette, but after one drag I threw it away.

I am sure you have been in situations where you were disgusted with the taste of cigarettes and vowed never to smoke again. This was one of those situations. I crunched up the pack and told myself I was never going to smoke again if I got through this. Two minutes later my friend returned and 45 minutes later I was in an operating room.

At this point you may be thinking that all you have to do now is to have a nasty accident and smoke some sickening cigarettes and then you will never smoke again. But all of you smokers know from your own experiences that however horrible those cigarettes tasted, they were not going to be my last. Like any smoker, the first thing I did after the operation was over and the anaesthetic had worn off was to find a nurse with a wheelchair and a pack of cigarettes (it is amazing how many health workers smoke) and get them to drag me outside for a smoke. Because I had not smoked for over 20 hours at that point, I thought that this cigarette tasted like heaven. My body was obviously uncomfortably low on nicotine and the irritable itch just needed a bigger scratch.

Uncomfortable situations

We have all been in uncomfortable situations and felt a need to smoke extra cigarettes. It may have been something more uncomfortable or upsetting than my motorcycle crash, or something more frustrating, like having to wait in the rain for a recovery vehicle or a bus that is very late. But smoking or not smoking does not change the situation you are in. Do not forget that you also smoke more when you are happy; you smoke more when you are bored; you smoke more when you cannot think of anything else to do; you smoke more when you are drunk; you smoke more when you sit on the toilet; you smoke more when you worry that you are smoking too much. If you carry on smoking, you will inevitably smoke more as your body needs a stronger fix.

However bad a day you are having, life is so much better without smoking. You have this false impression imprinted on your brain that makes you believe that when things are not going well it is time for a smoke. What you should be starting to realize is that smoking compounds whatever problems you are having. In fact, smoking might be causing some of the problems. Once you have stopped smoking, however bad things get you cannot help but enjoy the fact that you do not have to smoke. I smoked for well over half my life and even though I stopped 12 years ago I still pat myself on the back when I remember that I do not smoke.

Last week I experienced one of those desperate situations where I might have been forgiven for having the odd cigarette. Regardless of whether I would have been one of the world's biggest hypocrites, as a smoker you would have let me off this once. No one would have called me an idiot or a fool. They would have assumed that 'let him have what he wants'. I asked Sue if she minded if I told this story and she said if it could help make a point then she did not mind.

One of the worst days of my life happened a few weeks ago. My wife had to be rushed into hospital and have immediate surgery. At the time she was away from home so I jumped on my motorbike and made the four-hour journey to Devon in two and a half hours. Just before the operation the doctor came and told me what was going to happen and then warned me of the things that could possibly go wrong. That was when I felt the need to sit down and remind myself to breathe. When Sue was wheeled into the operating theatre I was trying to be strong but, as you know from earlier in this book, that is not me. During the operation we lost our unborn child and Sue, whom I love more than life itself, had to have parts of her anatomy removed. It was three hours before I saw her again and I went and joined all the many smokers outside the entrance to the hospital; even though smoking is on the decline, they still need a full-time cleaner just to deal with all the butts that pile up outside the hospital.

At that particular point in my life this book was the furthest thought from my mind and I did not care if the whole world took up smoking as long as Sue was all right. After what I was going through, you surely would have understood if I had asked a fellow smoker for a spare cigarette. While I was sitting outside the hospital you could not help but notice all the patients, visitors, anxious relatives and staff coming out for their much-needed fix. Even the patients who had bothered to put on their own clothes were still recognizable as patients, first because of the tags on their wrist and secondly because of the funny-looking socks they make you wear these days to cut down on circulatory problems caused by spending so much time in bed; hospitals provide these long, white, tight socks to improve the circulation to your extremities. At the time I first sat down, there was a large gentleman smoking who was obviously a patient, not only on account of his wrist tag and socks but also because he was dragging his IV drip trolley with him, with everything still connected to him. I could not help but wonder whether, if he had been given his lungs to carry in a plastic bag, he would still be out there smoking. I reckon he would.

About an hour later I was still outside the hospital entrance making phone calls to let people know what was happening and to cancel work, when from the entrance of the hospital trundled a frail, bent figure. It was an old lady making for the railings outside the front door at the speed of one mile a week. There were all the tell-tale signs that she was a patient: dressing gown, white socks, wrist tag, IV trolley with heart monitor and a pack of unopened cigarettes. Even most of the heavy smokers stared at her in disbelief. It took her two minutes to get a cigarette out of the pack and then she lit up. After the first drag on her cigarette she started coughing but by the fourth puff she was bent over the railings trying not to pass out. People asked if she was all right and she told them politely not to worry about her as she had been doing it for years (no joke intended). By the sixth puff she had had enough and before her heart monitor

blew a fuse she made her way back into the hospital. I swear that if it were not for having the trolley to hold on to she would not have made it into the hospital. She almost had an air about of her of 'I needed that'.

Two hours after seeing that old lady I was at my wife's bedside, holding her hand as she came round. Sue is one of the strongest people I know and in just over two weeks she was back on her feet, making a full recovery. Compared to her, I am a weak-willed person who is just about holding on to my wayward emotions. When I first stepped out of the hospital to get some air and make some calls, even though it was the last thing on my mind I could not help saying to myself 'At least I don't have to do that', referring to all the people who were smoking. At that precise moment in my life the thought did not fill me with joy, but there was a sense of relief that I could sit and deal with the situation with a clear head and without the distraction of needing to smoke.

You will always have bad days. That is a given in life. The way you deal with those experiences and how you move on from them will determine whether your life gets better or worse or stays the same. Many of us think that if we had our time again, we would do things differently. Perhaps we would have moved abroad, married a different partner, taken a more risky job, worked harder at school, or not started smoking. You can learn from the past but you need to live in the present. You need to know that however bad your day is turning out, smoking will only make it worse. Chemically it is going to affect your ability to deal with an already awkward situation and mentally it is going to make you weaker. Physically it is going to destroy your dreams of the future. If you smoke, your future is going to involve those grey clouds of fear, as you seem to find it harder to stop smoking. Smoking is not the one enjoyable vice that you can still do. It is a chemical trap that you just happen to fall into without realizing it. When you know what you want in your life, you will know that however bad things get, smoking is the last thing you will ever want to do.

Solution 24

We all have bad days; smoking cigarettes makes them worse. How we deal with those days determines our future; not how much we smoke.

25

The OFI syndrome

When discussing different types of people, many people use the terms A and B, or hunter and gatherer, leader and follower, risk-taker and non-risk-taker. I like to describe the different types as people with the OFI syndrome and people without it. The OFI syndrome is for people who, when confronted with certain dilemmas, instead of doing the sensible or practical thing choose to say 'Oh, f**k it' and take the more risky option. This syndrome is not necessarily a bad thing. If you look back through history, we are indebted to many people who said OFI and took a chance. Even in prehistoric times you can imagine that there were cave-dwellers who debated who was going to be the first to try this 'fire' idea. Let me give you some examples.

Think of Christopher Columbus. Everyone around him is telling him it's a suicide mission and he is going to fall off the edge of the earth. Did he decide to call it a day and go home for tea? No! He said OFI and shouted to his men, 'Set sail and bring me my extra-large compass'.

How about that Armstrong chap who was first on the moon? They were probably drawing straws in the shuttle for who was going to risk being the first to set foot on the surface. Even though he pulled the short straw, he could still have said 'no'.

Emmeline Pankhurst was at the forefront of the suffragette movement and helped to pave the way for equal rights for women. When she was planning to chain herself to the railings, don't you think she had to choose whether to take a set of keys for the handcuffs? What did she do? She said OFI, threw the keys away and then took the extra-thick handcuffs.

One of my great heroes as a kid was the great motorcycle stuntman Evel Knievel. You can imagine his manager asking him on one of his big show days, 'Well, Evel, is it going to be 20 cars today or shall we give those buses a go?' For those of you who might not know, he jumped the buses.

Many great people (you included?) have had to follow risky but ultimately profitable courses of action to further themselves and help others. We all make mistakes, but sometimes it is only by taking the risky option and making

mistakes that we learn what we are really capable of. One of the big mistakes all we smokers made, often at an early age, was to have that second cigarette. If we had just smoked the first one and realized that it made us uncomfortable and left us with an empty feeling, then we would have been smoke-free. Millions of people try smoking but never take it up; they have a few puffs, don't enjoy it and never go back to it. What did we do? We went back and tried it again and again without realizing the full consequences. We were not scared or worried about the other 60,000 cigarettes that might follow that second or third smoke. We were too busy trying not to choke or take all the smoke down.

If you are trying to work out whether you suffer from the OFI syndrome, let's look at some other scenarios where you might have had to choose.

▶ Your best friend rings you and tells you that he and his partner are getting married in two weeks' time in the Bahamas and they would love you to be there, but they will understand if you can't make it. You need the Thursday and Friday off to make a decent weekend of it but have used up all of your annual leave. Do you sit at home and think of the money you saved by not going, or do you ring up work and claim to be sick as you pack the suntan lotion?

▶ You are 15 years old and have some big exams coming up at school. But on Wednesday night next week your favourite band are playing an extra gig and your friend has a spare ticket. If your parents find out you are off at some wild bash, they will throw a fit. Do you say you are going to sleep over at your friend's house to study, but actually pack some extra clothes to change into before you go to see the band; or do you get the books out in your bedroom and say to yourself, 'There will always be another tour'?

▶ You have booked a fantastic holiday for your family and are driving back from the travel agent, very happy with yourself. Suddenly there is a loud bang from the engine and clouds of grey smoke are billowing out of the exhaust. You manage to crawl to your local garage, where Honest John, your mechanic, estimates the bill for repairs at £200 more than the money you have just spent on your holiday. You know that if you ring the travel agent now you can get most of your money back. Do you make the call or do you smile and think how happy your family will be on holiday as you look to see the limit on your credit card?

▶ Everyone has warned you about the boss at work. You know it's a cliché and you know that it will end badly, but you've always found him (or her) very attractive. So when the boss offers you breakfast at their place, do you explain that you like your coffee very hot in the morning or do you laugh it off and say that you have to go home and feed your pet hamster.

▶ You have a presentation to make the next day and your plan for that evening is to go over some of the work and get an early night. At the station on the way home you meet an old friend who you have not seen in ages. The friend is going to a great party and tells you that there will be other people there that you would love to catch up with. Do you go with the friend or say that tonight you must go home and work?

There is not necessarily a right or wrong answer to these questions. You are not a better or a worse person if you are always taking the riskier option. Much depends upon your temperament and the particular circumstances. If you are the type of person who is more tempted to say OFI and jump in feet first, clearly you like to take a bit of a gamble or a risk sometimes. With all the situations above, there is some real gain to be had from taking the riskier option, along with a price to pay at the end.

With smoking you might have said to yourself: 'I know it's dangerous but the risk and cost to my life and health are worth the pleasure I get from having a cigarette.' But saying OFI in relation to smoking does not work because there is no benefit or reward. Let's say you have stayed off the weed for a while, but people have still been offering you cigarettes because they do not realize that you have stopped or they want you back on their sinking ship. If you were to say OFI, take one and start smoking again, where would be the excitement of the risk or the gamble? Carrying on smoking is not a gamble; it's a dead cert. The dead cert is that tobacco will control you and it will choose how you live part of your life.

Acting according to instinct and emotions, rather than to caution and reason may be a blessing or a curse. But whether or not you adopt an OFI attitude when faced with making a decision, as far as smoking is concerned you should change the 'it' in OFI to 'that'. Lighting up another cigarette takes you down a road where there is no extra high or exciting risk or pleasurable reward. Just an annoying pain that cannot be satisfied.

Solution 25

If you are a person who acts on emotions and gut feelings, isn't it going to be great when you give up smoking and can enjoy real sensations rather than chemical cravings?

26

You choose

You will truly be in control of smoking when you choose to smoke your last cigarette. It will be the first time that you really are able to choose in your relationship with smoking. With all that you now know, you can never go back to using all the excuses that you used to justify your smoking previously. If you carry on smoking you are not living your life the way you want to; you are living a life that is dictated by tobacco companies whose only concern is whether your lungs will hold out long enough to buy another pack of cigarettes.

The only way you can ever get back to feeling content is not to have the next cigarette. The only time you have recently felt like a non-smoker is when you were smoking because that was the only time that you were relieving the craving. Even if you read this book with no intention of stopping smoking, you cannot go back to being the ignorant smoker that you once were. If you did, it would mean that you want to die early, you like feeling empty, you crave being a slave and you enjoy being conned and ripped off. Do you want your skin to age quickly? Do you want to get out of breath every time you walk up some stairs? Do you like paying for the privilege of making part of your life miserable? Will you lie on your deathbed and wish that you had smoked more rather than less, or will you lie there and look at smoking as one of the problems that you never got around to sorting out?

Whoever you are and whatever you do in life, you can choose to make things better for yourself and for the people around you. You may be doing some things already, but you know that you will do them better and for longer as a non-smoker, and you will also have more confidence and energy. At least as an ex-smoker you will not have that grey cloud of doubt and fear sitting over your head.

Too easy

Most people find the first few weeks of not smoking much easier than they had expected. There is often a sensation of why did I wait so long? What was all the fuss about? Or, I could have done this easily years ago. Remember that you have had to come on a journey to get yourself this far and you need to remember how you got here. You may be using the blank pages at the back of this book to highlight the points that are most relevant to you, or perhaps you feel they are lodged in your brain already. Many of you will have invented or created your own little sayings or stories that relate to you. If you write them down, they can be used to encourage others and yourself in the future.

A little warning

This might sound patronizing, but once you have smoked your last cigarette, always remember not to smoke again. That means never, ever, putting a cigarette or any form of nicotine in your system again. If you found stopping smoking easy, don't let it take away your healthy fear of smoking. Even people who do not smoke have a healthy fear of tobacco and its products. That is why non-smokers never say 'Yes, please' when someone offers them a smoke. If you recharge your nicotine brain by smoking another cigarette, you open up your brain to be fooled once more. Then the whole process of having to clear out the rubbish from your body starts again. That means you need to turn back to page 1 and begin once more.

You will have to deal with an initial withdrawal period, which is what you have been dealing with all your life as a smoker. It will soon pass and then you are left to deal with your brain's associations with smoking. For many, the initial part of stopping smoking has its own buzz. This is because you are initially in a fight and as long as you keep landing the right punches with your answers, you are never going to lose. Every time you knock out another part of your nicotine brain, you feel better and you are on a natural high. You will notice everything is a bit fresher in every way. Your fight becomes so easy that you end up sitting on your opponent and forgetting that they are there. Be careful! The novelty may wear off, and if you are someone like me who suffers from the occasional OFI syndrome, you need to be on your guard in the first few months. Never forget what smoking did to you.

Feel free to gloat

If you are like me, then your last cigarette can't help but be an exciting situation. You are entering a stage of life you have not experienced for a long time. There is a sense of freedom that you

have been missing, and a feeling of sharpness and clarity that has never been so vivid as it is now. Try not to rub it in smokers' faces, but you will find it hard not to smile to yourself when you see people with a cigarette hanging out of their mouths. It's not that you are laughing at them; it's as if you are laughing at the fact that you had to put yourself through all that grief just because your brain was short of a little important information.

Solution 26

You never chose to carry on smoking after the first few cigarettes; the drug in the tobacco did that for you. The good news is: you did choose to stop.

27

Breaking the chain

Whenever you want to change something in your life, you need to take that first step. Until recently you might have viewed smoking as just a habit that you needed to stop. As you now know, it is a chemical addiction that is perpetuated by the act of smoking. You should think of all the cigarettes that you would smoke in the future as a chain pulling you towards your early grave. Once you have put out your last cigarette, you break the chain and it carries on pulling without you being tied to the end of it. As that chain disappears off into the distance, your cravings for tobacco cease. If you have not worked out what the taking of an addictive drug really means, that chain will always be dangling around your feet just waiting to trip you up.

We discussed earlier how some people wished there was a bigger comedown from smoking when they stopped. This would mean that every smoker who quit would know when it was all over and could count the days it took before they felt free. Some say it only takes four days and others describe feeling the withdrawal pangs for up to three weeks. This may depend on how long you smoked for and how active you are. If you run around a great deal, your metabolism will clear the drug out of your system more quickly. If you are sedentary it may take longer. Dealing with the chemical withdrawal symptoms will not be difficult if your mind is in the right state. But even though it can be very easy to stop smoking, it does not hurt to go into the process well-armed. This chapter looks at some of the pitfalls that may trip you up and how to avoid them.

Booze

As smokers, and drinkers, we have all done it at some point. It was going so well. You have not smoked for a week-and-a-half and you are telling everyone that you have cracked it. For example, you are at a party at a friend's house and you have commented on how much better your beer or wine tastes without smoking. Other smokers have heard this and unconsciously check that they have extra smokes with which to supply you later. You have a bit of food and a couple more drinks and are very pleased with yourself for not smoking. You even comment to yourself how easy it is. Three people have already offered you a cigarette and you have politely turned them down. They even find your confidence a little arrogant.

During the evening your nicotine brain has been nudging you every so often and you have replied with all the right answers. Answers such as:

▶ Thank God, I do not have to do that any more.

▶ Doesn't it feel great not to have to smoke?

▶ Me a slave? I think not.

▶ Those tobacco companies can stick it where the sun doesn't shine.

▶ Look at those poor smokers. I wish I could tell them how easy it was for me.

A couple more drinks and a dance around the living-room later and, if you are not thinking straight (and how many of us are after a few drinks?), the questions and answers to your nicotine brain are not sounding as confident.

▶ I am in control of my body and I can do what I like.

▶ Having one cigarette does not make me a smoker.

▶ Ah, go on then, I will have just the one.

▶ Where is that guy who was smoking the Marlboro Reds?

Before you realize it you are having your first cigarette for a while. There is a tiny hit as you top up your levels and then you spend the rest of that smoke wondering why you bothered. You are in no doubt that you do not even like smoking and you are sure you will never smoke again. Unfortunately, as most of us know, you are now at the stage where you are tying that chain of cigarettes with a double knot around your neck. The chances are that if you have access to cigarettes, you will smoke a couple more that evening. Your smoking brain is now back in control and for the moment your common sense in relation to smoking has gone flying out the window. Your fellow smokers smile to themselves and nod their heads when you tell them that this does not mean you are back on the cigarettes because this time you chose to smoke.

Probably, you just had one drink too many or made a one-off mistake but, either way, now you are going to have to deal with that annoying withdrawal period at some point. For many of you, the next day will not seem much of a hardship because you know that you can go without a smoke. The problem is if you keep doing this every so often – drinking too much and smoking as a result – you will start to believe you are in control, and before you know it you will be a full-time smoker again.

If you wake up the next morning and remember that you smoked, try to be angry with yourself and tell yourself what an idiot you have been to smoke again. You do not need to tell anyone else or make a big thing of it. You know it was something that you did not want to do, just as no one likes to trip up and fall flat on their face. Give yourself a kick and accept that you may have to deal with those nagging cravings for a while longer.

Ideally, in the first month of quitting smoking try not to go out and get sloshed, and also try not to rub the fact that you have stopped smoking into the faces of people who still smoke. They will be the first people to offer you a smoke later in the evening, especially if you have pointed out how stupid it was to smoke in the first place. That's a bit like telling all your smoking friends they are ignorant fools who enjoy setting light to their lungs and are only one step from being junkies. No one likes to be told they are wrong, and no one is going to listen to the person who has just stopped smoking. The only people who are in control of smoking are non-smokers. When you truly reach that state, you can go out and get as hammered as you like without the fear of smoking again.

As we all know, when we are tipsy or drunk we tend to let our inhibitions go a little, while at the same time thinking of ourselves as more capable than we actually are. And as all smokers know, in this over-relaxed state it is much easier to smoke three times as many cigarettes as normal. This could be due to the diluting of nicotine in our bloodstream, but also to the deadening of the pain receptors in the back of our throats. If we are really drunk, we do not feel the harshness of the smoke on our throat. We all feel a lot more invincible or confident about ourselves after a few drinks, so why should we worry about dying from a few thousand extra cigarettes?

When I sit outside a pub these days and smell the smoke, I still find myself thinking, 'I'm glad I do not have to live with that anymore'. I do not let it bother me if friends around me are smoking, but if I am with friends who are non-smokers I will choose to sit in a non-smoking area. Something you notice immediately when you stop smoking is how much your clothes and hair stink when you have spent time in a smoky environment. Or how your clothes reek of cigarettes when you put them in the washing machine. I often wonder how anyone of the opposite sex ever came near me unless they smoked themselves or had a blocked nose.

In the first few weeks and months after stopping smoking you need to have the phrases and comments that relate to you firmly in your head. They are the tools you need to deal with the times in your life that you previously associated with smoking. In time, in just the same way that you became conditioned into having a smoking brain, you will have a non-smoking brain. The difference this time, though, is that what you are telling yourself now is the truth about smoking, whereas before your brain was tricked into telling you that you liked something, but only to relieve the pain that it had already created. If you think of smoking as being brainwashed, then think of your true views on smoking as a brain clear-up.

Accept the bad days

There will always be those bad days when you are not getting on so well. In the early stages of stopping smoking your reaction will be to think about having a smoke, because that is what you have always done in the past. You might even find yourself saying that because you fancy a smoke, that in no way means you have to have one. The best way to describe this situation is with the idea that it is your old programming kicking in on automatic. The plus point to the negative situation of thinking for a second that you want to light up is that you know that you are much better off as a non-smoker having a bad day than a smoker having a bad day.

You have smoke on the brain

I think about smoking every day. Not because I am writing this book or because I work with a lot of smokers. As an ex-smoker you will always look at smoking in a different way from a person who has never smoked. This is not because you wander around in a state of fear that you will suddenly start smoking again. It is because you have experienced what it is like to be a smoker and you do not want to do it again. This is no different from the feeling you have if you have ever had an accident while driving or tripped up on a pavement. You know what happens if you flick the nose of a frightened barking dog. It bites your hand! If you can think back to when you learned to ride a bike or climb trees, at some point you fell off or over and that is why you were more careful next time. You got better at riding and climbing because you did not want to hurt yourself. I remember the first time that I burned myself on the stainless steel kettle at home. It was a big, round electric kettle and I was waiting for it to boil to make my mum a cup of tea. While waiting I noticed that as I put my face, and especially my nose, closer to the kettle my face got bigger and looked funny. So I kept moving my face closer to and then back away from the kettle. You have probably guessed what I did next. Yes, I put my nose on a boiling, metal kettle. I looked a right plonker at school for the next few days, with a big blister on my nose. To this day I always remember not to get too close to a boiling kettle, whatever material it is made of, because of that learning experience. Once you have learned that a certain action has the potential to be very dangerous, you consciously or subconsciously remind yourself not to do it again. Do you ever forget to brake when you see a red light?

Every time you answer those doubting questions from your old smoking brain, you are getting stronger and better at being a non-smoker, until one day you hardly notice it. You know that crossing the road is dangerous and that is why you tell yourself to look both ways before you cross the road. You know that smoking is not part of your future, so every once in a while you have to look out for it trying to trip you up.

Holidays

Quite a few people tell me that they will pack up smoking after their holiday. For many, part of this idea relates to drinking alcohol, as most of us drink more on holiday. Remember that the biggest stress about a holiday is coming back. It's when you come back from a holiday that you really feel stressed. When you are on holiday you can do what you want and you are in control of what you do. You are at your most relaxed and carefree, so in reality it is a great time to stop, just like any other.

Part of the reason that I am saying this is that if you are not going on holiday for another month or two and you are going to wait all that time before you stop, your non-smoking brain might have been subdued by your smoking brain. This means that the whole process of stopping smoking is going to drag on for longer than it needs to. If you are a smoker reading this book and you are not smoking at this moment, then light one up now before you carry on.

Now that you are smoking, how frightening is it for you to imagine this being your last cigarette? Does that idea fill you with dread or excitement? With what you know about smoking, what would you miss? If you think about it, surely the time that you make the decision to smoke your last cigarette will not be some sacrificial experience. You will not be puffing extra hard and salivating over every last draw in the hope that you will never smoke again. Think of one real reason you need to carry on smoking. Millions of other people have stopped smoking and actually enjoyed the tiny inconvenience of the withdrawal period.

The time to stop smoking is when it is clear in your head what smoking has done for you. Not two weeks after you get back from holiday or a week after Christmas. If you take the information you now have stored in your brain and choose not to act on it immediately, it is like having a winning lottery ticket and leaving it in an old jacket pocket. Sooner or later you are going to want to use that ticket. Why wait to collect your prize when it is already there for you now? Compared to the life you have been living under smoking, stopping is like having a Christmas present every day. Not being a smoker is going to be that part of your life that you will really enjoy!

Solution 27

Never forget what smoking did for you, and never forget how good it feels not to be a smoker.

28

The last meal

As you may have found already when previously trying to quit smoking, the after-dinner cigarette is very tempting, especially if you have had a few drinks as well. Even though we have already discussed the association between smoking and food, you must be clear that sometimes your smoking memory will kick in, especially when you see someone across the table light up. For a second or two your brain may automatically say, 'I fancy one of those'. Don't panic; it is to be expected.

Remember that the empty sensation of craving a cigarette can seem similar to the empty sensation of feeling hungry. If you have just eaten a decent-sized meal, especially if it is a mix of carbohydrates and proteins, then it is normal for your blood sugar level to drop and for you to have a craving for sugar as your body seeks energy to aid with digestion. That is to say, for a little while after eating a meal you may have an empty feeling until your body can start absorbing the nutrients and energy from the food you ate. This is particularly true of the last, and usually largest, meal of the day when your body tends to be in a less active state.

Think of times when you have eaten a large roast dinner with all the trimmings: roast potatoes, cabbage, carrots, chicken, stuffing, parsnips, gravy and whatever else takes your fancy. After eating a big meal like that, you would think that there is no way you could feel empty or hungry for something sweet. So why is it that within ten minutes of finishing that big meal, when presented with treacle sponge and custard or four flavours of Ben & Jerry's, you feel the urge to have two helpings and contemplate a third? If you were to wait half an hour or so, the temptation to polish off two desserts would be much reduced. Your body is under pressure after a big meal as it is using a lot of energy to digest the food. The slight empty feeling is our brain's way of saying, 'Give me some energy quickly'. It is not saying 'Have a couple of smokes and everything will be better'.

It is not that you have to sit there waiting for your food to go down and say to yourself, 'This is not a craving for a smoke, this is not a craving for a smoke'. But every so often you may need to remind yourself what that empty feeling really is. It's the body saying: 'If you stuff loads of different foods down your throat, you are going to have an empty sensation as your blood sugar directs its energy to your stomach.' While it's doing that, you can sit back and enjoy the meal you have just eaten and plan your attack on the dessert trolley at a later stage in the evening.

This association with smoking will often be highlighted if someone nearby has just lit up a cigarette. It is no coincidence that the first few distant whiffs of a freshly lit cigarette actually smell nice. I have come across many people who have not and never would smoke, but who like the distant smell of a newly lit cigarette. My aunt used to enjoy the smell of my stepfather filling his pipe so much that my stepfather gave her a half-filled tin so she could enjoy the smell. That sounds a little weird but everything put into tobacco is designed to be enticing, as any good company aims to make its products. My aunt never took up smoking a pipe; she just liked the smell of fresh tobacco. So don't worry if you sniff some cigarette smoke and briefly enjoy the smell of it, because millions of other people do and they have never wanted to smoke in their lives.

Any time you get that after-meal sensation, give your brain the answer it needs. That empty sensation is your body craving some more food and the faint smell of smoke is designed to smell nice, just like a scented candle or a fragrance. If the smoke came from people either side of you chain-smoking while you finished off your meal, I doubt that it would smell that great, but from a distance it can smell nice.

Solution 28

That empty feeling after your meal is your body reminding you that it needs to digest food, not the signal to set fire to your taste buds.

The faint smell of a cigarette is designed to smell pleasant; millions of non-smokers think so.

29

Enjoy the ride

Many of you reading this book have been at this stage of your smoking career before. You have either smoked your last cigarette or are going to very soon. In the past, your attitude towards this event has been with a slight sense of trepidation or maybe a feeling of doom and gloom. That is not the case this time, as you know that you are giving up nothing and have everything to gain. By the time you reach this part of the book you know that smoking is something you never wanted to do and need never do again.

In the past, you might only have lasted three days and not even got past the withdrawal period, or you might have lasted three years only to find yourself back at the end of a cigarette or cigar. This time is different because you have all the answers to the questions that your smoking brain might throw at you, and all you have to do is remember them. I hope that you have used the blank pages at the end of the book to highlight the points that help to release you from your excuses for smoking. You may have even created your own adaptations of the points brought up by this book, which is great. Maybe these mental prompts are firmly lodged in your head or you have them written on your phone or fridge door. In the beginning it is very useful to have either this book or some other storage device handy so that you can turn to your notes if your brain needs a little reminder.

In this chapter I have included a few helpful exercises or commonsense things to do to help you on your way. You may feel some are not necessary or suitable, but it does not hurt to have a little assistance on your journey and to make the next couple of weeks even more comfortable and enjoyable. The reason I say enjoyable is that you never have to want or need a cigarette ever again; for your body, mind and confidence, that is an exciting and uplifting sensation. Saying 'No, thank you' when someone offers you a cigarette because you know you are no longer a smoker can be a real buzz; for some it lasts a while, for others it lasts a lifetime.

Visualization

If you have a creative and imaginative mind, this can be a useful aid. Try to imagine your nicotine withdrawal sensations as an actual character. For me it would be the child catcher from the film *Chitty Chitty Bang Bang*, as I found this character rather scary and evil when I was a kid. You may like to think of something or somebody else that you find frightening or distasteful. Whatever monster or character you choose, it's helpful if you give them some sort of character and voice in your head. Then in the beginning when you have these little cravings for nicotine, you can imagine the character sitting on your shoulder with their annoying voice, or you can think of them trying to crawl out of the back of your throat telling you its time to have a cigarette. (A little word of advice, do not shout out loud when talking to them, as you might find no one wants to sit next to you on the bus.) Each time they cry out for a smoke, answer them with a resounding, 'NOT FOR ME, THANK YOU'. Each time you give that reply, they will start to decrease in size, until very soon they fall off your shoulder because there is nothing to hold on to or they fall down the back of your throat and get swallowed up. It is hard not to enjoy telling them to go and take a running jump, and every day it gets even easier and more enjoyable.

Do something to lift your mood

In the first three or four days of stopping smoking there can be a particular sense of anxiety and emptiness. You need to do everything you can to put yourself in the best mood possible and to deal with any highs or lows that come your way. Picking some days that you can reasonably control is always a good idea. Monday morning as your start day for stopping smoking can be tough, as for many that day always begins with a sense of mild stress and anxiety. If you have a Monday to Friday job, I consider Wednesday evening a good time to start. You have got into the swing of work, you have a good idea of what is going on until Friday, the weekend is in sight and you can plan the weekend to suit your needs. Once you have not smoked for four days the nicotine is out of your system and each day becomes much easier. For those who like a drink, it will be easier to lay off the booze on a work night, and the clean feeling you get by stopping smoking may encourage you to abstain from drinking over the weekend.

The strongest chemical cravings for a cigarette tend to come in the first two hours and three days after your last hit. That is the time when nicotine levels are running low and then leaving the body. On the third day your unhelpful drug is clinging to your leg in the hope that you will not kick it off the cliff into its own chasm of emptiness. Remember to have some sort of plan because 'If you rely on your mood, you're screwed'. That evening, make sure that you have control of your time and fill it with any positive endeavour that does not resemble a mood-altering drug, and also allow time to get to bed early. If you find it hard to go to bed early, try to do something physical that tires you out. You need to get a good night's sleep so that you wake up feeling fresh in the morning. In the last few hours of the evening, destroy any cigarettes in the house and plan to enjoy the rest of the evening.

Here are a few suggestions.

- Organize your top ten pieces of music and listen to them.

- Watch your favourite movie or video clip.

- Go for a walk.

- Ring your best friend.

- Use your hot tub, or borrow your neighbour's.

- Demand as much sex from your partner as is humanly possible.

- Go for a swim.

- Relax in the bath.

- Read an interesting book.

- Play the guitar or whatever is at hand.

- Get out on your bicycle.

- Book a holiday.

- Write poetry.

- Sign up for that course.

- Go to the gym.

- Join a gym (you can afford it now you don't smoke).

- Play games with your kids.

- Get that yoga DVD out of the cupboard.

- Do something that makes you smile.

- All of the above (but leave something for tomorrow).

Whatever you do, do something, anything rather than moping around thinking about wanting a cigarette.

Music can be the most portable of mood enhancers so make use of it first thing in the morning when you expect to have to deal with a craving for nicotine. As mentioned earlier in the book, eating well makes a great difference to how you feel, so plan those foods that not only taste great but also leave you feeling good and full of energy. Try not to let yourself get hungry, thirsty or tired and if you do, acknowledge that and deal with it. Many people let themselves get dehydrated and often mistake thirst for hunger, thus putting undue stress on their bodies. You do not want that at any time and especially over the next few days. Have those phrases/strategies or a diary with you and if you find it useful, write down and express the challenges that you are going through.

Key point

Failing to plan is planning to fail.

Do everything you can to put yourself in the best situation.

Walking

Besides the obvious health benefits of going for a short, brisk walk, there is also another plus point to be gained from pounding the streets or park. Even if you are active and fit, going for a walk can help you to follow the easy path to putting up with any withdrawal sensations. When you plan to go for a walk, even though it might be for just ten minutes, you are planning to do something positive with your body and you can achieve it without any obstacles. You are moving forward and you can see the way ahead. Most of us think better on our feet and can see things more clearly when we are moving in a planned direction. This is particularly useful later in the day or evening, times that you previously associated with lazing on the sofa with a stinking cigarette and the ashtray resting on your stomach. If it is not possible to hit the streets, you could walk around the garden or run up and down the stairs ten times. At least that will show you what your lungs are for, but do be careful!

Breathing

You are quite experienced at this already, of course, but some simple, focused breathing exercises can be a great way of relaxing your mind and body whether you smoke or not. This exercise can be practised almost anywhere, but for the first few times it is nice to do it lying down. When you are used to it, you can do it standing or sitting as long as you keep your spine upright and do not slump or slouch.

Lie down on the floor on your back and place a hand on your tummy as you completely let your stomach muscles relax. Now take a big, slow breath in through your nose and feel your stomach rise and then fall as you gently let the air out through your mouth. Once you are happy with your abdominal breathing, put both your hands on your ribcage – just beneath your chest – so that when you breathe you can feel your hands moving outwards as you breathe into your ribcage. Again, once you are happy with this slow breathing into your ribcage, put one of your hands in the centre of your chest and breathe slowly and feel the chest gently rise as you fill with air and then sink as you release the air from your mouth. Do not force the breathing by pushing the chest or stomach out. Just keep it long and slow; you will not hyperventilate.

Once you feel you have controlled your breathing into each of these areas, put one hand on your stomach and one hand lightly on your chest. Now breathe in, filling up your belly slowly and as you carry on breathing in feel your ribcage expand and then your chest gently rise. When you feel full of air, release the air out through your mouth. See if you can count to 12 while breathing in and out; if you get to 12, start at one again.

This could last five to ten minutes, or longer if you want it to. It will help you to focus on using your lungs to make your body feel good, which is completely the opposite of what smoking does. It will also help to take your mind away from other thoughts as you concentrate on getting yourself into a more relaxed situation, which is much better than hurting yourself and making your body more anxious. As I said, you do not have to be lying down or even put your hands on your body; just try not to let your head drop if you are standing up or sitting down. So, if you are having a bad day and you only stopped smoking a few days ago, you could just sit somewhere with your eyes closed and take five minutes to get some air and help your body. The fact that you no longer smoke means that you are already better off than you were last week, whatever the day brings.

Key point

Do something to lift your mood.

Quitting smoking is an enjoyable step to a fitter future.

Smoking diary

Writing a diary may not be quite up your street. You may have to make a real effort in order to communicate better with yourself. But the diary will provide a conscious way of dealing with the out-of-date unconscious smoker that you were. Think of those times when you say to yourself 'I just want it'. Record them. That mood tends to come when you feel that you are not getting what you want in other areas of your life. Something like: 'I'm not getting the appreciation', 'I'm not getting the love', 'I'm not getting the breaks', 'I'm not being listened to', 'I can't have that and they do not want me', 'Do you know what? I can have a cigarette and I do not care whether I should have one, I just want it'. What's interesting in those situations is that we think the cigarette is our friend, but now you know it just adds to the feeling of anxiousness and insecurity.

Writing a diary, even if it is only for a week, will allow you to be honest with yourself. If you do trip up and let smoking back in, writing down how you feel will be useful to you in dealing with a similar situation next time.

Here is the first week of Sarah's diary.

Wednesday

7 p.m. Just finished dinner and had a smoke. Thought about throwing my cigarettes away but will just hold on till the end of the evening. Must go to bed early tonight.

8 p.m. Going for a walk and have left my cigarettes at home. I have a few thoughts in my head about smoking, the main one being getting a part of my life back and if not today then when?

9.15 p.m. They are in the bin and I am feeling a little apprehensive. I have been here many times before. I want to be smoke-free and I want to feel more in control. I am going to have a shower, jump into bed with my book and underline the most useful phrases that will help me tomorrow.

Thursday

9.10 a.m. Had some breakfast with the kids. Back home from school run and am working at home today. Didn't really think about smoking until now. I would normally have a coffee and a cigarette before logging on. The craving is not that strong, it's just a feeling of 'I fancy one'. Used the phrase 'I fancy one but I do not want all the other thousands that go with it'.

1.30 p.m. Kept busy doing the accounts this morning and avoided going outside for a smoke. I would not say that I am feeling confident but I do feel fresher. Had some lunch and a peppermint tea instead of a coffee. Went for a little walk up the hills and thought about how I need to do more exercise and that I was going to put all the money that I would have spent on smoking in a pot. This would be roughly five pounds a day.

3.30 p.m. Made some calls into the office to check some orders and now feel a little empty. Think I need a little treat so I am reminding myself 'That a treat is something that leaves me feeling good'. So I made myself a small fruit salad and that has sparked me up. Picking up the kids in half an hour and it will be nice not to have to change and freshen up because I stink of smoke.

9.00 p.m. Have to admit that once the kids had gone to bed my craving for a cigarette was really strong so I chose to do something that would help me rather than hurt me and went on the cross-trainer for half an hour. It was hard work but I felt really good and Peter made me feel even better by telling me how nice it was to go to bed with his beautiful fresh-smelling wife.

Friday

9.30 a.m. In the office today and have already avoided going outside with Belinda for a smoke. Have brought lots of fruit with me, and herbal teas to keep my sugar levels up.

2.00 p.m. Been out for lunch at the café and had a big cappuccino for a bit of a hit. Walked back with Belinda who offered me a cigarette. Did not make a big point of saying 'No' but I could not help look at her as she smoked and think how good it was to not have to do that. Hope I am not in danger of becoming some self-righteous anti-smoker. I am feeling a little pleased with myself but will not let it go to my head because I have been here before.

7.30 p.m. Drove home in traffic listening to Classic FM and felt OK. I would normally have smoked a couple of cigarettes in the car and it only popped in my mind once. Picked up kids from neighbours and they had already been fed so have not eaten yet and the temptation to have a glass of wine and a smoke is quite strong. Must not let my sugar levels get this low, so will have an apple and eat with Pete when he gets home. Will probably have a drink tomorrow as we have a babysitter and are going out for a meal.

10.30 p.m. Had tuna salad and Pete nearly passed out when I told him I was going on the cross-trainer again tonight. At this moment I feel really good and am sort of asking myself why I did not do this earlier. Still am a little anxious as when I feel this good I normally have to be a little bit bad to compensate. That would normally involve drinking and smoking. So let's see what tomorrow brings.

Saturday

10.30 a.m. Pete went swimming with the kids this morning and I did some jobs round the house. They won't be back for another hour so this is definitely a time I associate with smoking. Did pick up the smoking book and reread a couple of chapters. I am trying to keep my coffee intake down to two a day, to the ones I really enjoy, and must remember to take apples and bananas with me just to keep my sugar levels up. So far, so good.

4.00 p.m. Just got back from shopping and going to the park. Did catch a few pleasant smells of people smoking in the distance. It's strange I never noticed that before. It reminded me of a phrase from a film Pete likes, when one character says to another that sewer rat may taste like pumpkin pie but he wouldn't eat the filthy motherf—er. I wonder whether that odour of cigarettes is always going to smell nice? I just have to associate it with the truth. Smoking always leaves me dissatisfied.

7.00 p.m. Going out tonight for a meal and a few drinks and need to be a little bit careful. I'm going to do the things that make me feel good. Will let you know how I did in the morning

Sunday

10.00 a.m. Had a great night last night, may have drunk a little too much. I don't know if it was my imagination but the curry tasted even better than normal. Smoking did pop in my mind but only when I saw people going outside and to be honest I was glad that my evening was not interrupted by having to go out for a cigarette. I am feeling a bit fragile so I need to manage my stress levels so I can make the most of today. By now I would have already had three coffees and about four cigarettes. I am enjoying feeling cleaner. Pete in his own way is being encouraging and I feel I can hug my kids more without them thinking I stink. Had a good breakfast and am going to plan good food today rather than making an excuse for being hung-over.

7.30 p.m. We went to lunch with Peter's parents and my mother-in-law commented on how good I looked. I did not really want to mention the smoking as I do not want to make a big deal of it. Going to bed early and I would like to do some exercise tomorrow. I feel much better and I suppose because we all had such a good family day the smoking seemed very unimportant. Did slightly overdo the coffees today but I ate well and drank loads of water.

Monday

10.30 a.m. Had a good night's sleep and have just had a cup of tea with the smokers out the back of the office. Quite happily avoided the offer of a smoke. Looked at them smoking and I couldn't help feeling how much they needed every last deep drag of their cigarettes. I am not going to mention that I have had help with my stopping smoking; I am just saying that I am giving it a miss for the moment. Had to make it clear to Belinda that I am not pregnant, even though with the attention I am getting from Peter at the moment I will have to be careful.

2.00 p.m. Just back from lunch and I am definitely enjoying my food more. I am a little concerned how easy it seems to not smoke, must remind myself how low I used to feel as a smoker and to remember what I have been through to get to this point. I must not take my relationship for granted. (Hope that makes sense?)

10.00 p.m. Took Beth to dancing this evening as she does jazz and tap on a Monday evening. Made a point of taking my Kindle and some fruit, so I sat in the car and caught up with some reading. When I went into pick her up I couldn't help notice how much one of the mothers stank of smoke. Went on the cross-trainer for a quick fix and am going to jump in the bath before bed. I feel so much fresher already.

Tuesday

10.00 a.m. At work and I have to say I must be sleeping better because I nearly jumped out of bed this morning. I even had honey and lemon and a peppermint tea this morning rather than a coffee. Please do not ever let me go back to smoking. I honestly feel like I have more control over other areas of my life. I think because I am planning my food better my clothes feel looser on me.

3.00 p.m. Sat out with some friends at work while they smoked and I had to stop myself asking them why they were doing that.

8.00 p.m. It is official: I have swapped one addiction for another; I have just been on the cross-trainer for 40 minutes. Pete suggested I should use the money I am saving to join a gym; I don't know if I have time for that but I might enquire about some dance classes at the village hall. I am feeling calmer and even when there is a slight craving or association with smoking I find it easy to say to myself 'Why would I want to do that?'.

Wednesday

9.30 a.m. I am working from home today and a friend is coming over for lunch later. When it comes to not smoking I need to concentrate a little bit more when I am by myself. I don't know if it is boredom, loneliness or just the association I have with taking a break. If I feel a bit empty I will focus on getting on with something that stimulates me more. On a positive note, though, I jumped on the scales this morning and I have dropped 3 lb. It is not just the exercise; I think cutting back on all the coffee is really helping.

3.30 p.m. Went for a walk after lunch and thought about what we talked over the other day. In a way, not smoking has left a hole or you could say has given me more energy to do something else. At the moment I am just enjoying feeling clean, fresh, more in control and fitter but perhaps further on down the road I might like to do some work on fulfilling more of my values.

9.00 p.m. I took a rest from exercise this evening and would have to say that smoking was the last thing on my mind. I do feel I have been more mindful today, not in a melancholy way but a positive way. I do feel a little emotional so am going to drag Pete to bed for a cuddle. I would like to keep the diary going and maybe catch up next week for a chat. I have to say, though, so far so good.

Sarah wrote this diary a few months ago. She looks great and is enjoying a new sense of confidence in her body and personality. She still wonders why she did not make the change earlier and told me she never realized how crap she had felt until she felt this good. She is happy being a non-smoker and it's time you were the same.

Solution 29

Give yourself the life you deserve.

Keep a diary to keep you conscious.

30

Making a difference

Many problems exist in the world today – wars, terrorism, starvation, the destruction of the planet. By comparison, smoking may seem less threatening. Nevertheless, each year cigarettes kill more people than bullets. Can we do anything about it? Can we help to change the course of history? Powerful forces are in place. The tobacco industry employs millions of people. In fact, if you include the people who sell cigarettes, cigars and other tobacco in shops and in the street, the total comes to about 100 million people around the world. Tobacco products and sales feature strongly in the economies of many countries. Some political parties, and even governments, are partly funded by powerful tobacco institutions. I am neither anti-government nor anti-business but I am definitely pro-life and personal responsibility.

Many of us, and I certainly include myself in this category, have the tendency to be selfish. We put ourselves first and concentrate on what benefits us and makes us feel good. But there are levels of self-interest. Consider the following questions.

▶ How many of you reading this book would get a job with a company if you knew that the main effect of their product was to harm people?

▶ How many of you would feel happy knowing that your example as a smoker was influencing young children to take up smoking?

▶ How many of you would encourage other human beings to smoke?

If your answer to any of these questions is 'I would', please feel free to forget this book. Perhaps even see if you can get yourself up to smoking 100 cigarettes a day. Good luck!

Smoking is not the biggest problem facing our people or planet, but it is part of the selfish and thoughtless society and environment in which we live. The message of this book is that apart from those who have a vested interest in tobacco production and sales, there is no real profit or pleasure for anyone in smoking. The message of this chapter is that we may all be able to make a difference.

The old truism 'Bad things happen when good people do nothing' is relevant here. In this instance we all can do something. For example:

- parents and grandparents can set an example by not smoking themselves and by insisting that their own homes are smoke-free zones

- writers can use their talents to open the minds of many to the slavery of smoking

- teachers can set an example by not smoking themselves and by ensuring that pupils and students are made aware of the dangers of smoking through both the formal curriculum and extra-curricular activities

- ex-smokers can warn others of the dangers and expense involved in becoming a smoker

- famous people who have influence with the media can take time to encourage others, especially the young, to stay away from smoking

- governments can set an example by means of legislation to ensure that public places, including restaurants and pubs, are smoke-free and by the withdrawal of any subsidies or protection from tobacco producers

- farmers who produce tobacco can switch to other crops

- shops that sell tobacco can stop doing so.

Even non-smokers may find some of these comments over the top, but most smokers and ex-smokers acknowledge how much effort is needed to combat the problem. They also know how important it is to do so. No one chooses to smoke and be fooled by its cunning, addictive drug. Not one person reading this book would start smoking if they had their life again. So why should we allow smoking blatantly to take away parts of people's lives, especially when all tobacco companies target the young and immature?

Solution 30

If you'd known before you started smoking what you know now, you would never have smoked, even with someone else's lung, let alone your own.

Final reminder

Suppose I told you that you had a nut allergy and that if you ate a nut it would make your whole throat swell up and you would suffocate and die. What would be the one thing that you must avoid? Nuts. That's right. So if I told you that you will have a real problem if you put any nicotine in your system, what is the one thing you must avoid doing? Right again.

No substitutes

Smoking has been the tool of choice for the delivery of nicotine into your bloodstream. Until now you have seen it as the bringer of pleasure, but it has turned out to be the complete opposite. If you wear nicotine patches, chew the gum or suck on the little plastic inhalers (how sad does that look?), you are just prolonging the pain of smoking. Where do you think the nicotine comes from that they put in the smoking substitute?

The day someone came up with the idea of nicotine substitutes, the tobacco companies must have laughed their heads off, all the way back to the bank. Their business is to keep you hooked and all these different devices are just alternative methods of keeping you addicted to nicotine. Any attempt to wean yourself off it bit by bit while keeping the drug in your system prolongs the agony and sends the wrong message to your brain. The real message to send to your brain, the message of this book, is that you are fed up with being tricked by this drug and you are not going to put up with it any longer.

I have listed in the next section all the key points and solutions that have been highlighted throughout the book. There are also some blank pages so that you can add key points of your own. The next stage, once you have stopped smoking, is to think of ways in which you can help others who also want to stop smoking. As the old saying goes: 'You can buy your friend a drink, but first they have to walk into the pub.' I will let you work that one out for yourself.

Key points and Solutions

▶ When do you want your life to start getting better?

▶ If you rely on your mood, you are screwed.

▶ When you get to the point of realizing you never want to smoke again, you almost want to bottle the sensation, it is such a pleasurable feeling.

▶ You should be the one making choices in your life, not some unrewarding drug that costs you an arm and possibly a leg.

▶ Smoking is literally like a cloud obscuring your senses; once you stop, you can enjoy the clarity of life you deserve.

▶ Nicotine is not a drug you take by choice; it is a clever substance that perpetuates your need for it.

▶ To regain your control, you need to realize that the tobacco companies have been controlling you.

▶ The only real enjoyment that you will ever get from smoking is when you stop.

▶ Before you started smoking you were content and never suffered cravings or a sense of emptiness. Once you clear the nicotine out of your system, that feeling of contentment returns.

▶ If the tobacco companies force-fed you camel droppings with nicotine in them, you would end up thinking you liked them.

▶ You lose the empty feeling of needing a cigarette when you stop putting nicotine in your system. You lose the desire to smoke when you realize that smoking creates that empty feeling.

▶ Does your next action hurt you or help you?

▶ Do the things that honestly leave you fulfilled. Realize that the important things in life are not things.

▶ Hands up those of you who in any way trust the companies that have been supplying you with your tobacco.

- Once your brain has answers to all the excuses, all you need to do is use it.

- Give your mind the right answers and you will get the right reactions. Without the nicotine in your system, your old nicotine brain has nothing to hold on to.

- By updating your faulty smoking brain, you are living a more honest experience.

- We all have to go sometime, but how you live your life determines how happy you are when you die.

- If you carry on smoking, you are already standing in front of a bus; it's just not here yet.

- No one, especially children, thinks that they will be the ones to die from smoking, but no one likes being fooled at the expense of their health, money and freedom of choice.

- You either smoke or you do not; smoke one cigarette and it leads to another and another and another, and so on.

- Every so often your brain will say, 'I fancy having just one cigarette'; just remember that you do not want the other 50,000 cigarettes that go with it.

- The biggest saving is your sanity from the madness of smoking, but the money also comes in handy.

- When you are stressed by a particular situation, you need to do something to make that situation change and move forward. Smoking just adds more discomfort to an already uncomfortable situation.

- History shows that scientific evidence about the harmful effects of smoking has led to a dramatic decline in the numbers of smokers in several countries, including the UK and USA.

- Better sex; healthier babies.

- Any attempt to limit or control your nicotine intake highlights the fact that you are never in control of smoking. If you carry on smoking, it carries on dictating your life.

- Whatever age you are, now is the time to say that you are fed up with being conned by tobacco companies and their clever chemical trick.

- There is a reason to eat and that is what makes you hungry. There is no reason to smoke.

- Choose the foods that lift your mood.

- We all have bad days; smoking cigarettes makes them worse. How we deal with those days determines our future; not how much we smoke.

- If you are a person who acts on emotions and gut feelings, isn't it going to be great when you give up smoking and can enjoy real sensations rather than chemical cravings?

- You never chose to carry on smoking after the first few cigarettes; the drug in the tobacco did that for you. The good news is: you did choose to stop.

- Never forget what smoking did for you, and never forget how good it feels not to be a smoker.

- That empty feeling after a meal is your body reminding you that it needs to digest food, not the signal to set fire to your taste buds.

- The faint smell of a cigarette is designed to smell pleasant; millions of non-smokers think so.

- Failing to plan is planning to fail.

- Do everything to put yourself in the best situation.

- Do something to lift your mood.

- Quitting smoking is an enjoyable step to a fitter future

- Give yourself the life you deserve.

- Keep a diary to keep you conscious.

- If you'd known before you started smoking what you know now, you would never have smoked, even with someone else's lung, let alone your own.

Your answers to why you never need to smoke again

....
....
....
....
....
....
....
....
....
....
....
....
....
....
....
....
....
....
....
....
....
....

Index